SHORE LINES

WORD-PICTURES
FROM AN ISLAND

First published in 2019 by Acair, An Tosgan, Seaforth Road, Stornoway, Isle of Lewis, Scotland HS1 2SD

www.acairbooks.com

info@acairbooks.com

Cover and interior design by Catriona MacIver for Acair.

A CIP catalogue record for this title is available from the British Library.

Printed by Hobbs, Hampshire, England.

ISBN: 978-1-78907-016-3

Registered Charity SC047866

Shore Lines

Word-Pictures From An Island

BY

Donald E. Meek

For
Sophia, Evie and Lachlan

CONTENTS

INTRODUCTION

This collection of verse is not intended to present 'poetry' to the reader. Its contents seldom qualify as such, if they do at all. Rather, it is meant to preserve a record of how one person from one Hebridean island has perceived his native place, its people and its cultures, over more than sixty years. It can be regarded as a set of windows on past and present, an album of word-pictures of scenes, contexts and personalities, a kaleidoscope of changing perceptions, moods and emotions.

These pictures have been drawn or painted over the last decade or so, when I began to contemplate writing an 'autobiography'. In fact, I found it easier to think 'pictorially', to recollect subjects individually, and to fashion each set of thoughts as a 'poem' or at least within a poetic frame which defined the boundaries of that set. The thoughts vary, and so do the frames, from popular song tunes and doggerel metres to blank verse.

Whatever form suited the mood of the moment was pressed into service. I am not a writer in the sense that I spend time consciously seeking inspiration or toiling with style. I am not 'full-time' in any literary or literal sense. My thoughts control me, and not vice versa. I write down what forms in my brain during the day or night – and I have often had to leave my bed in the early hours to catch the passing thought, and record it on my keyboard. What I get at such times is what you see here, with very little enhancement beyond the first draft.

Today, in 2018, the population of Tiree is very different from what it was in the early 1950s when I was growing up. Many of the population are 'incomers', as tends to happen never-endingly with islands, or they are hybrids (and a Gaelic speaker called 'Meek' should know). They come at different stages in their lives, often with their minds well formed, their perceptions already shaped by previous experiences.

1

As a Gaelic-speaking native of Tiree in all but place of birth (which was Rotten Row Maternity Hospital, Glasgow), I like to feel that I saw the island 'from within', and that my views of island life have their own validity. These views are probably very different from those of the 'new' population, and they may find it instructive to take a look at the island through the other end of the lens, so to speak, and through other eyes.

My island is not one of glorious sunsets and sunrises, of holidays and 'opt-outs'. It is an island of close contact with the soil, with crofts, horses, tractors, boats, fellow islanders, struggling to live in challenging conditions. It is an island of winds and storms, of rough edges and hard choices.

The island has shaped me to the extent that, in spite of living on the mainland to pursue my education and former academic calling over forty years, I am still an islander. I relate to it as I sit here and type this in Falkirk, just as I have related to it over a lifetime. I am a detached piece of the rocks and machair which I describe in some of my verses.

I have retained a close connection with Tiree throughout my life. I helped to maintain the family croft until the end of the 1980s, travelling backwards and forwards as required, usually at times of holiday. During the 1990s and the early 2000s, Rachel, my long-suffering wife, and I toiled to clear the old holding, make it fit for another generation, and above all to preserve the family home, 'Coll View', now happily occupied and splendidly renovated by our elder daughter, Rhoda, who has taken over the croft.

Such a dual existence – academic and crofter – was not easy by any means, and often generated moods of anger and frustration, unknown to the summer visitor or the 'incomer', who begins where he or she stands. I had to deal with the baggage (and rubbish) of generations, both physical and emotional. And yet, in spite of that challenge – which has driven many others away from their native islands – the old bonds of loyalty held firm.

Living away from the island has also made me different from those who have remained in Tiree all their lives. I see the island in frames very different from theirs, and I struggle – in a way which they probably do not – to accommodate the immense changes in its culture which have occurred since 1950. I return as the 'native', only to feel that I am an exile in my own island. The emotional challenges are not hidden here, though often tinged with humour.

Some things remain unchanged, however. My love of boats, ships and aircraft, generously nurtured by many boyhood visits to the mainland, has not diminished in any way. An affection for horses and tractors has endured. The island's contours, and especially its shorelines, still hold me in thrall, as I have watched them and walked them on many different occasions. I have composed many lines of verse, in Gaelic and English, on these walks.

Above all, I am comfortable with living in Tiree and on the mainland – a legacy of those early days when I needed treatment for my 'lazy eye' from the age of two, and had to go to Glasgow Eye Infirmary every six weeks. Oban and Glasgow, accessible by transport, feature prominently in this set of pictures of 'my island', then and now. They are an integral part of my concept of being an islander, an islander with 'dual nationality', so to speak.

In collecting my word-pictures in this book, I hope that others will find them of interest, and I will be delighted if, through my efforts, they appreciate more fully what it has meant, and means, to me to be a native of Tiree.

Donald E. Meek
Falkirk and Tiree, Spring 2019

INTRODUCTION

SOUND

PERSPECTIVES

CAOLAS

That long straggle of houses
Now white against blue water,
Edged with humped islands
Below far horizons of hazed hills,
Fringes my perception
From Miodar to Àird Deas:

No, that is my outward eye,
For my inner eye knows
It forms my understandings
Of past, present and future,
Worlds yet to be discovered,
Townships already known:

Its narrow name releases that
Current of creative energy,
Mighty kilowatts of power
Sufficient to illumine millions,
Driving my mind and hand
Even when the tide
Is on the ebb
And Gunna
And Coll
Vanish.

SCENE FROM CAOLAS

(For Kenneth Steven.)

Mull is a clouded vertical triangle
Above a valance of green cliffs:

Iona is a miniature chest of treasure
Jewelled on the snout of the Ross;

The Treshinish Isles are stepping-stones
Flat from the Cailleach Bheur's creel;

Jura is a swelling of blue breasts
On a misty levitation of gentle heat;

Coll is a rugged mouth of white lips
With craggy ears on a pitted face;

Gunna is a slantwise crocodile
Lying low to chew the sound;

Greasamul is a tufting of grass
On a ruffled parcel of rock;

Rum is a deep pouring of hill
On melting ridges of sunset;

The Small Isles are a heady cocktail
Of shining stone diluted with seas;

Barra is a humped sea-monster
With a lighted head flashing firm;

Skye is a mountainous mouth-organ
Playing distant tunes at evening.

SOUND ORIGINS

I am, of course, a child of Gunna Sound,
Somehow struggling ashore aeons ago
Amoeba-like, finding a foothold,
Little claws on soft sand,
Between Greasamul and the Clach Ùl,
And groping upwards to land and light,
Beyond the Port Ruadh,
Reaching warmth and new being
But never fully of the machair,
Left stranded on a raised beach
With that hankering after a receding ocean
That pulls me inexorably
To the tides and currents,
The ships and boats struggling in turgid turmoil
Or gliding on tranquil translucence
Between the two Caolases.

My origin lies millennia
Behind that great rending
Flood that tore and filled a trench
Breaking one island into two,
Bursting angrily over massive rocks,
Submerging a fault, a fracture in the surface
Of the known world, a thunderous dissolution
Shredding and remaking by the ferocious forces
Of earth's creative turmoils.

Somehow I transformed westwards
From fish to land creature, processing,
Hanging grimly on to the end
Of an anchorless biological chain.

Or was it thus? I lived and moved
And had my being in Gunna Sound,
Long before I knew it?

Times I walked Ceann Tràigh Thòisinis
Looking for that clear message, glittering in a bottle,
To explain causality! But I did not find it
On the million, million particles,
The complexities that fit together firmly,
Enjoined to perform their tasks, their interactions
Above, below, around, beside, within
This maelstrom that forms me –
And all humanity.

I am the agnostic of the rational,
The atheist in scientific method,
Who crawls not towards the physical,
But to a realm beyond the disputatious
And tempestuous tides and currents
Which rule that uncertain Sound of the intellect,
Finding firmer understanding of self
Shrouded in deeper,
Diviner mysteries.

STONE AGE

Again that row of stones
Gathered by little hands
From Tiree shorelines
Sits along our wall,
In shapely palaeolithic beauty.

We all gathered
These jewels, lifting them,
Feeling their shapes,
Putting them in our pockets.

As we walked the shores,
Some went unconsciously
Into our souls. They made
Our walk uncomfortable
And different.

I rediscover mine regularly,
Examine, explore,
Splinters, pebbles,
The occasional boulder
That somehow levitated
And lodged mysteriously
In my inside pocket,
Near my heart,
Like the huge Clach Ùl
At the Port Ruadh,
Remnant of an Ice Age
When Gunna Sound
Was chiselled out?

I don't want to dress them,
Polish them, smooth
Their rugged contours:

No, I'd rather return them,
Drop them gratefully
Back along my path,
And let others
Pick them up.

SHORE LINES

FINDING THE WORDS

ADJECTIVES FOR MY ISLAND

Adjectives for my island
Cling rigidly to cold rocks,
Fossilised limpets
Unwilling to rise,
Definitions solidly
True-bonded,
Robustly real,
Recognisable,
Foundational,
Immovable.

I try to wrench them
Off the grudging gneiss
But nothing yields:
They belong there;
I know I must resort
To explosive energy
Of a higher order
To blast them out
Metaphorically,
Metamorphically.

I want to find
Solid formations
For my constructs,
Words welded in furnaces
Of primordial creation,
When lava flows
Were blazing oceans
In geological faults
Cooled by Ice Ages,
When rocks folded
In easy undulations.

I do not want
Dead descriptors
Of soft seaweed
Lying by the ton
Washed up wantonly,
Anonymously,
On transient shores,
For surface skimmers
To gather them lightly
From superficial sand
For their mendacious
Melange.

BEACHCOMBING

This island of poetry
Is shored up with clichés;
I trample them, and then
They squawk around me,
Seagulls, oyster-catchers,
Their wings threadbare,
Their cries ever audible.

So much plastic garbage
Tossed overboard too
By consumerist bards,
Non-biodegradable,
Picked up by walkers
For every celebration,
As if nobody has ever
Seen such jetsam before.

Siren voices somewhere
On the far-away machairs
Recycle this old music;
When the insistent birds
Stop attacking my head,
I hear their wailings
In the ceaseless wind.

Where can I go to find
A new pair of eyes
Free from grey cataracts
To discover new words
On these clichéd shores?
To find fresh ears
Free from blockages
To hear sounds beyond
The old accustomed
Comforting noises
Of land and sea –
And dull humanity?

WORD STORMS

Lifeless calms do not move me,
Balmy days requiring no thought,
When clichés sail past Caolas
With white sails set to catch
Gentle stereotyped breezes,
Bedecked with delusion,
Rigged with common cordage,
Towing soft rubber boats
In a wake of unreality.

Rather my soul lives in storms
With powerful personalities, fresh
Proper nouns with bow thrusters
Conveying essential meanings,
Trying to berth in the tempestuous
Harbour of my deepest creativity,
Struggling to conquer currents
Swelling with wind-driven wrath,
Emotions raging in the Sound
Of white-flaming adjectives,
Forcing elemental participles
To show their truest syntax.

Then I feel my pulse:
Pugno ergo sum:
I fight: therefore
I exist.

IN AN ISLAND

I could not live on an island,
Standing there on top of it,
Precariously trying to grip it,
Robinson Crusoe on a raft,
Thor Hyerdahl drifting on *Kon Tiki*,
Passenger on a ferry,
Worker on an oil platform,
Aircraft on a carrier,
With mechanical prospect of take-off,
Steam catapult enabling lift
To false altitude.

I could not live on an island
When hurricanes swept eastwards;
Without grip or depth or substance,
Anchorless, light, transitional,
I would go with them,
A haystack unravelling,
Flying apart,
Fragmented,
I would be off it soon.

No! I have always lived
In an island,
In its sand, in its machairs,
In its caves, in its houses,
In its rhythms,
Tidal, human, natural,
In its ebbs and flows,
In its ups and downs,
Flat stretches, hills,
Mountains, moors –
I am in all of that.

And what's more, I'll tell you,
All of that is in me;
The rugged beauty is deep,
Lives inside my life,
I have the island within,
Dictating my contours,
My profile, the set of my bones,
My emotions, feelings,
Yes, and language,
And dialects, special words,
Songs, and music,
My way of being,
A mutual in-ness,
Holding fast.

Aye, you can always tell
The newcomers, without
The centuries-old rootedness,
The feelings of generations;
They live 'on an island',
'On Mull', 'on Coll', 'on Tiree',
But what of them will live on
And where?
How much will they leave,
Before they too move on?

My life is into the 'in',
Into the core of the earth,
Into the pliable magma below the ancient gneiss,
Into the most molten, immovable,
Renewable reductable rocks,
Generation after generation,
Going away, but, yes,
Coming back, knowing the meanings
Of gigantic two-letter words.
For me and for them
'On' is not 'in'!

FINDING THE WORDS

Rock And Soul

ISLANDER

Geology, not genealogy,
Is what makes an islander:

The body-mass is multi-layered,
Metamorphic, forced into shape
By prehistoric immensities,
Compelled to adapt irresistibly:
Sedimentary, receiving deposits
From rivers, mountains, seas
Of all kinds for millennia,
The levels lying deep,
Contorted into patterns,
Fossils of ichthyosaurs
Indelibly implanted:
Igneous, occasionally spewing fire
In the face of cold indifference,
Welcoming Vulcan's power
Within the soul of being,
Impatient with stratification,
Trying to release magma,
Never keen to let matters rest,
Always prepared to enjoy
A self-created earthquake,
Ready for the next tsunami.

The summit is weather-beaten,
Showing signs of erosion,
Glaciated mercilessly,
Storm-ripped, fault-lined,
Furrowed, crystallised,
Gabbro and schist protruding
Through dykes and cone-sheets,
Sharp central ridge, scree-sloped,
Heather-fringed lochs adjacent,
A massive gloup above
A determined headland.

An islander is rock-solid,
Immovable, impenetrable,
Unless you know how to drill
Through all the layers
To reach the hot core –
And find the switch!

PORT NAM BAIGHDEAG
('THE HARBOUR OF THE COWRIES')

Nobody in Caolas remembers your Gaelic name
Any more: I am the last survivor of the native stock
Who used to go there with wonder in my heart,
Amazement at the never-ending discoveries
Of fragile beauty battered by the ocean swells,
Driven through rocks and clefts and fissures,
Hammered and pounded by waves and storms,
Shovelled by the greatest earth-moving energies,
The massive water-powered JCBs on the perimeter of
the island,
Exerting mighty force, moving tons of sand and shells,
Pulling them back like seagulls' feathers,
Thrusting them forward, rolling them over,
Never stopping the ceaseless upheaval,
Reshaping the coastline, making it different,
Changing it with every tempestuous tide.

And yet, there you were, shimmering quietly
In the magnificent frailty of your fragility,
So small that you were strong beyond measure,
So weak that you could defy primordial forces,
So gentle that you were happy for this small boy
To pick you up, roll you over in the palm of his hand,
Take you home, and put you on display on the dresser,
In the full glory of your minute majesty.

Cowrie shells, you speak in your silence,
Above the roar of the never-dying storms,
Telling a story of endurance beyond our knowing,
A survival against every power unknown to man,
Except in its merest outline, its acceptable superficiality.

You made that harbour, Port nam Baighdeag,
What it will ever be for those of us with understanding,
And its name runs through my waking hours;
I will take it with me until I lie among the listening dead
In Kirkapol, the groaning of Gott Bay to my right,
And you will be in that performance somewhere,
Eternally resonant, the tiniest reminder of what matters
And of who I am, who we are,
In the weakness of our strength…

If only we could get back to where that boy
Stood in admiration, gazing into the palm of his hand
At the priceless jewels of the shoreline.

ROCK AND SOUL

GREASAMUL

Seeing you green-maned,
With white wave-crests
Rubbing your brown flanks
On a day of sharp skies,
We romantics would overpaint
Your stark nakedness, fill in
Your deep incisions, put
Poetic polyfilla in your cracks:
But to those who saw you
With penetrating essential eye
In history's cruel dawn,
You were no more than
'Humped island of grass'.

Precisely so, and thus you remain,
Joined to Tiree by tidal causeway,
Negotiable only at lowest ebb,
Defiant, dangerous, unreachable.

Your name-givers knew you well
When they spittingly eschewed
Flattery, faced razor-edged reality,
Discovered your summer value,
Thrashing some cattle across
That unpredictable neck to graze
Above your fractured valance.

Norsemen held life hard,
Did not leave their own lightly,
Brooked no soft sentiments,
Kept stark onomasticons,
Told it straight, lastingly,
Shoved nomenclature's sword
Down bloody Gaelic throats.

In golden evening sunlight,
We dream contemporary fantasy,
As the cold steel of the *Clansman*
Clatters intently southwards,
Kishmul's CalMac galley,
Swerving past the green buoy,
Red funnel roaring out grey fumes.

Her island-hoppers will not cast
Even a shrivelled glance at this
'Humped island of grass':
They have better hummocks
To behold.

CORMORANT

Still I am out on that headland
On a mauve morning
Hiding behind hard rock
Gouged by heavy tides
Playing a dangerous game
With humans, deceiving seabirds,
My cap waving softly to attract
The cormorant seeking a perch.

I blast with 12-bore precision
A shower of lead, and those black
Feathers flop into the swells,
Dog paddling out on heaving waves
To rescue the dead, to lay the carcase
Obediently at my feet.

Home I come warily,
Well taught by my father,
To watch officialdom.
We pluck the bird boldy
For a family feast.

The soup, the fried meat,
The delicious meal
Of seabird's flesh
Stays salt on my palate,
Still tingling sweetly
Fifty years later –

My conscience guiltless
Of cormorant's blood.

ROCK FISHING

I often stand there
On the steep ledges
Of an autumn afternoon,
Tide filling, wind gentle
On shore, the long rod
Vacant, nothing biting;
I throw the limpets
Crushed to mush,
Lift that rod again.

Sun dusts Calgary
In lazy October light
Falling headlong
On to a seal's snout.
Bad sign, that beast,
Looking askance
In a slow swell
Between us.

Razor of rock
Sharp on boot,
Pointless hook,
Not catching.

No red rock-cod
Here this afternoon,
No pink fins flapping
On dark gneiss.

Mist powders Coll,
Evening deepens
In long curves,
A shower caresses
Treshnish islands,
Fragile rainbow,
Smooth smirr
On my face.

I put the flexing rod
On my shaking shoulder,
Ease off pins and needles.
The seal is still there,
Rippling his whiskers
Gladly, as I leave
Homewards.

He does not know
What I have caught
In another ocean.

PASSING CAOLAS

My boat steers by landmarks,
Looks for the familiar alignments,
Takes instructions from rocks
In front of houses, converging
To guide the mind, as my hand
Instinctively turns the helm
Towards the safe passage:
No compass needed, no radar,
Only the feeling that land and eye
Are in alliance, while the heart
Feels a throb of kinship
With the elements, a deepness
Beyond knowing, as contours
Change into eternal verities.

SCARINISH HARBOUR

There is something
Deeply primordial
About this sharp cut
Through ancient rock:
Deftly designed from
World's foundation
To allow passage
Narrowly, carefully,
For harbour-starved
Hard-pressed seafarers.

Boats back from toil
Rest their souls
Here, sing gladly
In a choral fringe
From pier to inn,
As if completeness
Was wholly intended,
A generous harbour
But with no excess:

I sense it each time,
An essential sacredness
Of things surely meant
To be as they are,
Precisely, perfectly,
To test islanders
Of wide shorelines,
Make them appreciate
Exits and entrances,
Living and dying,

Coming and going,
Ends and beginnings.

Out there deep seas
Weave a tweed
Of natural tones,
Throwing a thread
Of sharp radiance
Through the cleft
To touch my eyes,
Lift my gaze.

This spring evening
In a mauve sunset
On an ebbing tide
Fishing-boats curl
Alongside each other
With orange floats
On blue hulls,
Creels ready
For tomorrow.

ROCK AND SOUL

THE REEF

This vast unending machair, sweeping
For ever through the flat island,
Through my mind too, unstopping,
My eyes without, within, trying
To hold this plain of history,
This undeniable centrality,
In meaningful balance
In its vastness
In my small self.

I cross the bridge from Baugh,
Blinking at the hugeness of it all,
As the stream flows under my journey,
River of boats and baptisms,
Of summer evenings with model yacht,
A crossing-point from east to west
And back again, and again, and again,
Filled with eternal initiations,
With preachings, powerful words
Still around, cutting my body
With rites of passage,
Boy to man,
Youth to age,
Birth to death.

Wartime remnants spike pastures,
Halifaxes, Hudsons, thundering,
Mighty hangars lowering hugely –
All still there somewhere, still visible
In rays of light far beyond my world:

This is a story universally greater
Than today's struggling Twin Otter
Tussled by strong gusts, touching
Tiny wheels on slanting cut-back runways.

I can still see it over there,
That camp where stranger and islander,
My mother and my father,
Met, talked, married, and became others,
Where part of me arrived in wartime,
And waited for the essential consummation
Of the moment for me to be.

Strange to think that. No island, no Reef,
No airport, no war, no me. That's the wonder
Of this machair of flourishing creation,
Its great magnetic sustenance,
Its massive fecundity, lying below
Levels of sea, levels of mind,
Levels of being, foundational,
Holding an island together,
Holding a world of meaning,
Holding life's mystery,
Still insoluble.
Why me?

LANGUAGES AND LEARNINGS

TRINITY OF TONGUES

When I opened my larynx
I found three tongues
All made to measure
The worlds in which I lived,
Each finding new words
To define my places
In life's linguistic universe.

Gaelic came first,
A strong, incessant tongue
That knew the rocks and hills,
The cows, the sheep, the dogs,
Flora down the road
With her cups of strong tea
And her fauna on the machair,
Far islands clad in mistery.
I spoke to past generations,
Travellers of the world,
Tellers of old stories,
Builders of new boats,
And then I found a family
Much larger than Tiree,
Irish, Welsh, Manx, Cornish, Breton,
Keys to other cultures.

English came second,
Language of 'making your way',
Meeting me ominously in school,
Then appearing in every book,
Jumping at me,
Forcing itself into my soul,

The teacher-cuckoo in the nest,
Shoving out the other chicks,
Building life's structures
Regardless,
The school an island of English
In an ocean of Gaelic.
English took me out –
But Gaelic took me in,
Kept me anchored,
Held me fast in raging,
Wrangling, wretching,
Wronging, ripping
Tides of hostility.

And out the door I went
To Glaschu, Glasgow, Gleska,
Where yon third lingo
Lived upon the street,
Spoken by the bunnets on the corners,
The wee folk wi bendy legs
And hearts so big
And minds so strong
That they built an Empire
Of ships and cranes and cars
And lorries and trains,
Put steam around the world,
Sewed railway tracks into fabric
As tough as granite,
With that deathless glint
Of Gleska humour.

LANGUAGES AND LEARNINGS

'Where's ye from, wee man,
Wi yer Gaelic twang?
Frae Tobbirmorey or Tiree?
See Davie there,
He's Hielan tae,
A teuchter like,
But he's some man, Big Davie,
An his behher hawf
Is Aggie, aye she's posh,
Speaks Emburra,
An her accent wud cut gless,
But, aww, they're awfy nice
Aw ma friens, aw o them.'

Gaelic, English and Gleska
Are all friends of mine,
Mo chàirdean gràdhach,
Teangannan mo ghaoil.

CLASSROOM CAPERS

Her stomach oscillates
In a bout of smoker's cough,
Nicotine forelock jumping
In anger at pupil's spelling,
Shaking on her high chair,
Waves of fury spilling over
Exposed wooden desks
As we snigger dangerously
Behind our blotted jotters,
Waiting to be keelhauled
Systematically for misbehaviour,
Misspelling, misunderstanding,
Mis-everything, in our abject
Ignorance of all things.

In the back row suddenly
Thunder sounds forth, maps
Tumbling off a cupboard top,
Dislodged by a capsizing desk,
Pupils covered in Mercator's
Projections as they unfurl
For yet another lesson
On the geography of Hell:
A pupil leaning backwards
Has lost his equilibrium.

We monkeys in the front row
Struggle with a storm of giggles,
Innocent of this catastrophe,
But knowing that there is
No escape as she explodes
For another happy day
In Ruaig School.

DOCTOR'S VISIT

In memory of Dr Catherine A. Brown.

Light shone as you entered,
White coat radiating brightness,
Your smile filling us with joy,
Your gracious motherly concern
Placing that steel-cold stethoscope
On our warm chests, allowing us
To listen to your gentle heart-beat
Pulsating with love for each of us,
Your annual visit an everlasting
Moment of deep reconnection
With the beauty of human life.
You filled the gap of compassion
In that hard, uncaring school,
Made us feel that we mattered.

When we met on the train
Between Glasgow and Oban
On that lingering last journey,
That same smile banished darkness
As you walked into the chill mist
Of that frosty Taynuilt night;
I knew I had been with an angel,
As the darkness was as light
On your way homewards –
And on mine.

Loch Etive's challenging glory
Lived deep wthin your soul,
Your father, Rev. Alexander,
Baptist preacher from Tiree,
Taking the Gospel light by boat
To all who lived along its shores,
Caring for their total welfare:
You brought that same light
To those under your care.

You suffered the little children
To come to you gladly,
And you blessed them.
That blessing lingers still,
Beloved Dr Catherine,
Physician supreme,
Lady of light.

END OF WASHING DAY

Blankets of memory
Wave eastwards in line,
Flapping wet rhythms
To rinsed clouds
On sky-blue cloth,
A breeze smelling
Of warm suds
Seeds ozone
Into the Sound.

Draughts whistle low
Between open doors,
Wind dries dripping floors,
Rugged washing boards
With glass corrugations
Lean supportively
Against a weary mangle,
Wooden tubs, zinc baths
Sit in drained purity,
Scrubbing-brushes
Relax tired bristles
As the boiler cools.

My weathered great-aunt
In flower-patterned overall
Laundered by storms
Steers the strong elements
To a knowing conclusion
With a winsome smile
And a Gaelic story
For the lad returning
Washed in school's
Alien soap.

SAMARKAND

An Orient Express
Filled full with dreams,
Camels and drivers,
Merchants in streams:

Silver-peaked mountains
That burst the blue sky:
No Taliban present –
Silk cloth out to dry:

As I make my journey
On Kennedy's bus,
And reach Cornaig School,
With all the day's fuss:

This morning it's English,
Two periods of style,
With Mr MacDougall –
It will last a long while:

But out of those poems
Flies the name 'Samarkand':
It bursts like a sunbeam
Through a very dark land:

And I'm off on that journey
On the far silken road,
Far away from Room Three,
No need for a goad:

I'm captured by magic,
By the sound 'Samarkand':
Each time I hear it,
I join that small band

Who are tuned to the splendour
Of words and their ways –
On that 'Golden Journey'
Till the end of my days.

FORMATION

I walked Gaelic fields
Where once youngsters played
With happy wholesome voices
In long evening shadows
Before masts appeared
On their mind's horizon –
And games stopped.

I walked shorelines too
With the squawk and squeak
Of swooping seabirds
Protesting against intrusion,
Calling to my deeper self
To preserve boundaries,
To walk warily, carefully,
Respectfully:

Waves roared foamingly
Against red-specked rocks
As the moorburn in Coll
Threw orange flames
Into the night sky:

And I felt the slow heat
Within that silent spring,
Sensing how easily
Cultures die.

KNOWLEDGE

It was in that damp box
In that big bleak room
That great-aunt Maggie held
The heart of the family:
She kept what mattered,
What would transform
That mildewed box
Into a lantern.

Only, she had to die
And, in dying, bequeath it
Beyond that coldness
To let it become amenable
To a gentle spark of fire
From another mind
That had not suffered
The pains of poverty,
The agonies of rejection,
The thanklessness of those
Whose lives she treasured,
But who saw no jewels.

Her hoard was golden
To understanding eyes:
Her gems of knowledge
Now safe in a castle,
While that mildewed box
In the big bleak room
Glows in film and print,
Prose and poetry
From my heart.

POLES AND POSTS

NOTES FOR THE JOURNEY

In the deepest darkness,
Music took me home,
No light but faint moon
Struggling with grey-black cloud,
No road to see,
No vision but chords
Of humming in the wires.

Each pole a friend
Bearing messages of goodwill,
A woodwind orchestra,
As the night breezes swept low
And played their melodies –
Deep bass from the pole with the bent back,
High soprano from that shapely trunk,
A happy purr from yon ancient tree,
That was now telling stories
To those younger friends
In lyrical line by the field's edge.

Spooks were set at bay,
But sometimes a tinkle
Broke the harmony,
Sent a shiver through my spine
As a folktale ghosted past,
A headless body buried in words
That only wind and poles remembered
In that atmospheric ceilidh-house
Of myriad rings.

I'd quicken pace,
Speak to each pole,
Asking distance,
And the tune would come,
Across the flattened machair,
Bleak miles shortened
Into consoling cadences,
The house gable now clear ahead,
Marked by the strong north pole
With tuneful cross-angled bars
Beside the red phonebox,
The melodeon of the heart
Filled with sounds and sweet airs,
Soft voices in an island
Full of telegraphic noises.

PHONE-BOX ON A GABLE

A phone-box, red-rusted relic,
Defines this house: not 'Coll View',
But 'the house with the kiosk
On the north gable. You can't miss it.'
Marker of identity for fifty years,
A centre of communication,
But so much more than that:
A heavy black receiver to report births,
Holidays, illnesses, deaths, marriages:
To transmit news too, to comment,
To share, to bare the soul in a secret
Confessional, as the wire-bearing
North pole howled deafeningly
In a crackling Storm Force 10,
Or on deep autumnal evenings,
When blind beetles took to flying noisily,
Crashing into the small glass panes,
Door ajar, held open with one foot,
Guff from stale fag-smoke suffocating us,
As the black beetles fell dead,
And old directories lost their covers,
Reduced to flakes by boiling heat
Alternating with Arctic air-currents,
Times greenhouse, times igloo.

It must be haunted, that box, by ghosts,
By lives, losses, loves, hates, hopes,
Favours, fears, delusions, deceptions,
Conveyed by wire through elements,
Hot lines, hot wires, hot tempers,
Cool characters, cold temperaments,
Blazing words that would melt copper,
Freezing put-downers on a hard cradle.

We learned our buttons in there,
Turning that letter-figured silver dial,
Pressing A, B to get us connected,
Or give us money back. There was even
A human operator to talk to us,
To share the gossip, to let the world
Know our message, keep tabs
On island ways. 'Delighted to hear
That Mary is coming home tomorrow.
Sorry that Seumas was stopped last night.
Nice to have a chat, John: now,
Could you put me through via Oban
To Pollok 614826. Thank you.'
'That's it, you're through…'
What the operator heard –
To be honest, I hate to think…

Oh, that phone-box on our gable end,
Its door slamming in the winter storm,
As our fire blazed up the chimney,
Its bell ringing through a summer evening,
When hay was being stacked, and sunsets

Were long, yellow, orange, dark-shadowed,
And we had to search for a possible
Recipient who had forgotten
A life-changing assignation.
Ach well, not important,
Another time.

But now, I want rid of the thing,
To get at my gable end, to communicate
With stone and concrete, blocked
By fifty years of other people's business.
It's time to ring eight bells on that kiosk,
To give it a message for itself,
'You've had more than your three minutes,
And I'm cutting you off.' I am indeed
A very grumpy operator.

Aye, that's what I want to do,
But that phone-box is more than metal:
It is identity, not merely for this house,
But for a township, an island, a world,
A holder of voices now gone silent.
If only I could listen again!
If only it could play them all back!
It was new and strange once,
But it's old now, familiar, even friendly,
Part of what makes us who we are,
A memory-store, a definition.

You see, in a place like this,
Substance is nothing:
Significance is all.

CAOLAS PILLAR-BOX

George Reigns in Caolas!
Still enthroned in stone and metal,
Red-faced, with a very small mouth
And a 'big spare' (before zips)
At the top of his constricted gut,
To permit his Royal Male servants
To open his stomach, peer inside,
Examine his vitals, where snails
Slither over his innards, leave trails
Of glinting silver, masticate letters
Into ragged-edged snail-mail.
Definitely mail, no femail organs here,
All very masculine, mean, macho.
The Royal equerries tidy up
His entrails every second day,
Make his office public,
Clean him out.

He presides indifferently over all,
Cares not for change in size
Or shape or significance
Of other people's business:
No, George Still Reigns Here
As he did on Day One,
And, my goodness, his rain
Has poured for almost a century:
Wet, wet, wet, I'd say: and
The Royal Mail is a damp squib,
If it comes from Caolas.

But, of course – and I do have to say this –
We, the poor serfs and bonds-people
Of this god-forsaken peripheral fringe,
Illiterate and incorrigible savages,
Were deeply blessed to receive his
Condescending attentive ministration
To our needs, as our distinguished ruler,
All twelve inches = one foot
Of his 'spare'. He allowed us to get
The subsidies, by filling in forms,
'Yes / No / Don't know / Coma co-dhiù',
And posting them off (via his paunch)
To the distant Department.
Kept us all in touch,
Generation, after
Generation.

His person is enshrined there forever,
Embossed for the boss – GR, GR.
And there's no denying, is there,
That he has served us well?
Long may he reign!

PROCESSING PAST

RECYCLING

No fly-tipping in those far-off days,
No 'No Dumping' notices,
No hint of prosecution
Down there by the Sound of Gunna,
Where the sea surged white
Tanging the air refreshingly,
Energetically waiting
For something more to chew.

The seapinks grew from ledges,
Defiant 'Daisies of the sea',
Clinging hard to cracks with yellow mosses,
Barnacles, limpets, whelks,
Brown, grey, black,
Light lichens too,
Deep down in the crevices.

We would arrive with the jute bag,
Clanking, rattling, tingling,
On Aunt Maggie's broad shoulder.
She would throw the first tin
Into the abyss – resoundingly,
A Heinz 57 once full of beans,
Paper fluttering off to meet the seagulls;
Then the oblong tins
Devoid now of salmon and corned beef;
Some HP bottles too,
Some broad flat specimens
Formerly powerful,
Now thrown hard by a little hand,
Learning how to smash glass

Against brutal rock –
Hissing, jingling, falling,
Bit by bit, fragment by fragment,
Into the unknown.

Stories came to life
Of those who rounded these rocks,
My aunt getting into her stride,
White headscarf flying over grey hair,
Patterned overall fluttering,
Forearms throwing heavier rubbish –
Any old iron, cogwheels, spent gear-chains –
Manfully into the sea.
'That's where Seumas's boat
Hit the rocks, but he managed to stuggle
Ashore…'

Sea now swirling with incoming tide,
Great surges of white foam flecked with blue,
Stirring the gravel, the cowries so fragile,
So beautiful, down there with metal
And glass, waiting for the great grinder
To make them yet again
Grains of metal, elements of sand,
Dust to dust.

PROCESSING PAST

I walk stubbornly home,
Souvenir cowries in hand,
Behind that great lady
Who knew the rise and fall of tides,
The crunching of the ocean
On life's rocks –
Animated but serene,
At one with the elements.

SPINNING-WHEEL

I have a happy memory
Of the day the skip arrived;
I'd been praying for a century
Because of my great pride

In being such a 'with-it' guy,
Who hated all that's old,
And couldn't stand those ancient things
That made my heart feel cold.

So, when I least expected it,
The darkened skies turned blue;
The yellow skip was sitting there;
The world could now be new.

I skipped along and looked around
The rubbish-littered croft;
Everything was 'for the out',
And I would not 'go soft'.

So first I took the implements,
The plough, the cart, the scythe,
And dumped them happily in the skip –
My tune was rather blithe.

The fencing wire was next in line,
And I rolled it from the fields,
Where it had lain for many years,
As iron never yields.

And it went in with twirling spires,
Ascending to the skies;
I filled that skip in half an hour,
And prayed for larger size.

And then I had two skips for fun,
And that was truly fine;
Old tools went whizzing out the door,
And yards of fishing line.

Washing machines and fridges too
That waited many years,
Toasters, cookers and old grates,
Iron bars and shears.

The rowing boat that went to fish
And sailed across the sound;
Its planks were rotting, so why keep
Such clutter on the ground?

And then I found a spinning-wheel,
And said, 'What earthly use,
Is this for us with our new ways
Of keeping clothes quite spruce?'

So in it went, wheel in the air,
And treadle breaking free;
It sat atop that glorious load,
And that was that for me.

And now the croft is sparkling clean,
No junk around the doors;
I look across the 'lawns', no less,
And think – 'The end of chores'.

But somehow that old wheel returns
And breaks my happy dream.
It speaks of something rather more
Than just a wooden beam.

Tradition there, and maybe skills,
To keep a family clad?
And Gaelic too, and happy song,
And life that once was glad?

The skips have gone, they'll not return,
Nor will the junk therein;
But, O, that spinning-wheel of mine –
Please give me one more spin!

THE OLD BAROMETER

I miss the old barometer
That hung within our hall;
It was fixed so firmly –
That 'glass' would seldom 'fall'!

Pressure rarely bothered it,
Or came within its range;
Its needle rested quietly,
And pointed us to CHANGE.

A hurricane of greatest strength
Like Betsy and her kind
Might move it down to STORMY,
But CHANGE it soon would find.

An anticyclone had to top
All those that yet had come,
Before the needle rose a touch,
To FAIR – that was the sum

Of the best weather it could tell,
Because it had a mind
To know that CHANGE would happen –
To truth it was not blind.

The many hands that touched the glass,
And tapped it in their day,
Have long since left this pressure zone,
And CHANGE has come to stay.

And CHANGE has come upon the wall
Where it so long held sway;
We threw it out, because we said,
'We need to CHANGE our way;

'We need precision, not a guess,
We need to know the bar,
The pressure means a lot to us –
It makes us who we are.

'We take delight in all the stress
That makes our wheels go round:
The ups and downs are what we want,
From highest 'high' to ground.

'We cannot live with CHANGE for all,
We want the STORMS and FAIR;
We much prefer extremes of life,
Real CHANGE must fill the air.'

That calm old glass is in the dump,
And I sure lament its loss;
It truly knew the ups and downs,
But CHANGE was aye its boss.

CROFTING LIVES

CROFT LIVING

Life is a croft, an untidy guddle,
A ragged patchwork, rocky sometimes,
Breaking plough-shares, smashing straight lines
Into fragments, furrows zig-zagged,
No sense of direction beyond the wind
Or storm in your face, trying to make
Progress against traditional reluctance,
Broken fences to be repaired everywhere.
At least you can stay on the surface
Occasionally.

But sometimes it's flat, deep-soiled, fertile,
Yielding, co-operating, offering promise,
But don't be deceived by fecundity.
There's a price to pay before reaping.

It asks for constant attention,
Making you its servant,
Demanding you as its seed,
Ploughing you hard into itself,
Harrowing you with its insistence,
Burying you in weeds, leaving you to struggle
Through the choking overgrowth,
Eventually poking your nose
Through the sinewy turf.

It consumes effort, it eats energy,
Sucks it right out of you,
Leaving you exposed to rain and sun,
Lying there, trying to find your essence
Before you are swept up, baled roundly
As silage for winter,
Ready for recycling,
Ready for spring.

FIELDS

How dead they lie beneath their winter shades
Of withered grass, broken rushes, blasted blades,
Where once I ploughed, and sowed, and rolled,
And saw the dust rise, clouding evening airs!
Harvests were there, with sheaves and stooks,
Ears of barley, weighted down with grain.

Waterlogged, with flooded drains, they're bog,
While geese, the favoured tenants of our age,
In massive flocks now graze them bare –
Environmentally correct, but humanely wrong;
Lands lie waste, where birds and animals reign.
This is a swamp, a nightmare preview of a day,
When none shall live here, but the wealthy few,
And nature rules supreme with deadly gaze.

But look – up there, upon the sunward brae,
The grass is green, and offers fertile hope!
That was where the township had its roots
In run-rig time, before new crofting came
To stem the tide and stop the endless drain.

How strange to see it now, a radiant field,
While dying acres lack the folk to care!

RECOLLECTION

They battled to keep control in those fields,
With blistered hands, hard tools, merciless
To human skin, on their knees thinning crops,
Giving them a hope of essential roots:
They asked for no excess, their frugal minds
Penetrating stone, knowing the layers,
The soil from which they came, earthy, friendly,
Cold, wet, dust-dry, seasonally adjusted
Like themselves, attuned, supporting
Meagre futures rich in life's meaning.

Today I walk among the fields, go round
The dykes and marches in memory,
Looking at outlines of furrows in sunset,
The deep, long lights and shadows playing
On underused hummocks, rough ridges.
I struggle to remember the boundaries,
As familiarity declines, reciting names
For ridges, hillocks, rocks, recalling
The effortlessness of leanly trained minds
Who knew exactly whence they came
And where they were going.

Few others care or know where I walk:
That's not relevant to their lives:
Their grand cultivation lies elsewhere,
Far beyond my simple patch:
I fumble anachronistically,
As bloated grasses of obscurity
Unknowingly
Kill contours.

CREAG A' MHANAICH 1964–2014

A smirr of rain on Creag a' Mhanaich,
A gentle smell of wet, rank grass,
As up the slope I stride with strength,
The latest set of boots to pass

This ancient way to check each march,
Each fence, each gate, each rocky mass,
For sheep and lambs that may have strayed
Beyond the confines of their class:

Life stretches on, as through the mist,
I walk alone, concealed at last:
Dreaming in my own small world,
The future calls me, not the past:

I walk once more that self-same slope,
Full fifty years of time amassed:
What I would give to stride with strength –
And lose that man whose form has passed!

MILTON ROAD

Where have those fifty years gone,
Since I walked the cows and stirks
Down that road to the common grazing
In summer mornings before school,
When the grass was fresh with morning dew,
And lark-song filled the air?

Then again in evening, school's boredom past,
The dog and I would have our adventure,
Searching for the far-spread herd,
Lost in purple heather, deep browns,
Or radiant greens in warm sunshine
Somewhere near Port Bàn.

The dog would sweep right out
To furthest edge, and at whistle's sound
Nip their heels to get them moving – faster, faster,
Through the shallow moorland lochs,
Disturbing moor-hens, water-hens, hares,
And hurling waves of spray sky-high,
As I would egg him on. He'd hitch
A lift on a cow's tail to take him over
That final loch, as udders swung
And legs kicked, and clegs bit.
Through the gate, and up the road
We'd go, a sluggish convoy, as cows chewed
The grassy verges, and I fell headlong
Into deep ditches, my bicycle wheels
Slipping on gravel, pitching me off.

Oh, those days of freedom, with nothing
To disturb my leisurely nomadic ways,
Beyond weary workers cycling home!
Today there are no cows to drive,
No bulging Ayrshire udders losing milk,
No swinging tails, with dung-splats in the air,
No inquisitive stirks nosing through fences,
No hooves crunching dusty rutted paths:
I have only two dogs to walk on leashes,
Sniffing the verdure, tugging me along.

But now I am the animal, being herded
Off the road by a stream of cars, never-ending,
My thoughts broken by the rumble
Of yet another set of wheels on tarmac:
I daren't relax, let myself wander:
Quickly I seek refuge on the ditch's edge,
Holding the dogs to let a shining vehicle
Hurtle uncaringly past
My lethargic memories.

TEA IN A HAYFIELD

My mother walks from the house
Over fallen swathes, basket swinging,
Puts it gently down, summons us,
Happy toilers in that fragrant field
In an afternoon heavy with heat
To partake of this natural eucharist.

Gladly below the wobbling stack,
Ferguson tractor temporarily silent,
We sit solemnly on the soft earth,
Remove our cloth caps reverently,
Unscrew the old flask to taste
The sweetest tea ever known,
Biscuits baked to perfection,
As bees float buzzing past,
Flies land dangerously on
Fingers tipped with butter,
Dogs come for their share
In this fleeting fellowship
Of elemental gratitude.

Where is that hayfield now,
That harvest of radiant summer,
That feast of simple sufficiency
Below heaven's harmonies?
Where is that settled weather?

Is it all a painting fondly faked,
A false memory of arcadia
To make life palatable
For the final reaping?

STACK-MAKING

Up here the world is wobbly,
Unsure, uncertain, will pitch you off,
Tramping down resistant hay,
Filled with freshness, springing back,
Ready to send headlong
The oppressor of nature's resilience,
While two-pronged fork relentlessly
Throws up load after load.

Round and round I go,
Dizzy with determination,
Loosing balance,
Stumbling on,
Lurching

Until I grip the ladder,
Reassuring wood firm,
Swing my leg round,
Stomach butterflying,
World still reeling,
And I stabilise
To descend.

The green sky
Looks very steep.

LAST STACKYARD
August 1976

That evening I felt its nudging,
A dark premonition in the sunset,
Second sight sensing in its glow
The finality of this gathering of stacks,
A sudden skelf spiking discomfort,
Pricking my peaceful pasture –
Go now, or lose an image
Demanding remembrance.

Knowingly I walk to view
A stackyard set gently alight
In the day's final exuberance;
I gaze at its golden swellings
Radiant on a distancing horizon
Of strong boyhood energies,
Heavy fork-loads dying warmly,
Yet reaching robustly across
The long evening shadows,
The ladder resting for the night,
Arms and feet no longer needed,
Fresh stacks settling slowly.

Cattle call inquisitively
Through fading light
In supportive sympathy,
Clatter noisily into frame,
Noticing my unexpected
Concern; as they bellow,
I close the last shutter.

Now I open it to look
At this elegy in colour,
A stackyard filled full
With a glorious harvest
Of undying gratitude.

AULD LANG TWINE

Should auld connections be forgot'
And never brought tae mind?
We'll spin a ball o' cordage yet
For love of binder twine!

For love of binder twine, my friends,
For love of binder twine,
It held our world together, folks,
Did dear old binder twine!

When Fergie's linch-pins fell away,
And them we could not find,
We'd tie the drawbar to the stays
With lengths of binder twine!

When gutters broke around the house,
And gushing streams would shine,
My father, he would always say,
'Let's get the binder twine!'

When braces snapped because of strain,
And dungarees declined,
We'd haul 'em high and keep 'em there
With good auld binder twine!

When gates had broken from the hinge,
And in came sheep and kine,
We'd put them back to swinging form
With lengths of binder twine!

When storms were raging out at sea,
And making walls of brine,
Our boats were anchored safe at port
With cords of binder twine!

For auld lang twine, my dears,
For auld lang twine,
We'll tie the knot o' kindness yet
With lengths of binder twine!

WORD CROFT

On this croft I grow
Crops of words,
Sown with care
And well weeded.

Down there, in the far field,
You can see my adjectives,
Ripening in the wheat
Of a productive day:

My nouns are in need
Of some thinning
To get rid of some properly
Abstract turn-ups:

My best verbs are already
In my sturdy stackyard:
I feed them as main crop
To my sentences,
Which grow grandly
In barren winters
In my creative poem-shed:

I scan their lines
Every morning to decide
Which can be taken
To the reading marts
As mature meaters.

Then I load my stock
Into a treacherous trailer
Towed sensitively sideways
By a fine-tuned Ferguson
To a famous festival
Where poem-drovers feel
My fattest specimens
And pass sentences.

I return impoverished,
Poor returns on hard effort –
But I am a crofter of words
And I expect nothing.

I hereby declare
That I have registered
My poetic croft.

HARNESSING
TRACTORS

ISLAND AUTUMN

Seals howl on far shores,
Young flopping white on sand,
Their cries caressing Gunna Sound,
As the horse eats brown dulse
And wet seaweed streams
Through old cart planks
On slippery Port Ruadh.

We heave ourselves homewards
Heavily over the machair,
Shafts creaking in shadows,
Harness chains clanking,
Progressing sideways
In slow groaning rhythm.

A ponderous black beetle
Drones like a Lancaster bomber,
Its wings too small,
Its steering cumbersome
As it collides with
My young forehead.

We reach next year's
Ordained potato patch;
I haul the wet weed
With bent grape
Off the broken boards.
It flops soggily
Over rubber boots.

Horse unharnessed,
I taste the dank evening
On salt adult lips.

POLLY

We cried bitter tears,
Spoke in low voices,
When Polly died that Sunday night,
Not cured by mash and water
Carried to her canvas shelter:
That fine mare was too tired
To relinquish her last rest,
Her days numbered
On the plate of SB 7711.

On Monday the Ferguson
Hauled her white body,
Tail fanning behind her,
On a sledge linked hard
By chain to its towbar,
Tugging mercilessly.

I see her still, passing
The smithy door,
Where she was shod
For heavy haulage
By my father's hand,
Now steering the tractor
To that massive grave.

I was there to witness
That mechanical send-off,
That indifferent hearse,
That ironic cortege,
That huge brown hole
On the soft green machair,
A full day's labour.

Sixty years later, pensively
I still visit Polly's grave,
Remembering the day
The petrol pony
Heaved the white horse
To her last home.

And now, proudly,
We nurse the pony.

FERGUSON TE-20

The mind that devised that tractor,
Clean, clear, purposeful,
Seeing essentials,
Eschewing superfluities,
Getting down to earth
With a plough lightly attached
For enlivening heavy soil,
Exposing the dark side to light,
Deepening land's fertility,
Reducing danger in encounters
With harsh geology,
Overcoming obstacles,
Bringing order on four wheels
With hydraulic pipes,
Lever-controlled,
Complexity made perfect
In simplicity. A singularity
Of practical multiplicities.

No time here for nonsense,
No time here for self-indulgence,
No time here for waste,
No time here for pomposity.
Just plain Harry, without
A redundant knighthood.

What use is a title
When a tractor needs true power,
Delivered by cylinders linked
To crankshaft and transmission,
Empowering transformation
Through three-point linkage?

The important people
Live at ground level.
'Ferguson' does the job,
Reigns supreme.

Genius on two feet, tall, slim,
Impatient Irishman,
Small head with massive brain,
Produced a miracle,
Diamond of engineering.

TE-HE-HE-20

I do not want a Jaguar,
An Audi or a Porsche,
A Lamborghini or a Bentley,
Or even a Rolls Royce.

I've no interest in status
Or travelling in style;
Bottom of range will do me
For covering a mile.

But a Fergie TE-20
Inspires my deepest joy;
For ploughing fields and pulling,
That surely is the boy!

The dungheap loves its loader
When lifting grim manure,
And it will haul the seaweed
With claws that are most sure.

And if you need a taxi
To reach the Co in time,
You can trust the grand wee Fergie –
Its comfort is sublime.

The luxurious hydraulic
Will hold your heavy tail,
And make your coccyx tremble –
The linkage will not fail.

As you cross the rocky moorland,
Your vertebrae will sing
A hymn of praise to Harry
For his super three-point sting!

So to pot with BM Dubya
And all these fancy things:
Just get a TE-20,
And you'll really spread your wings!

HARNESSING TRACTORS

HOMECOMING

Just to get home to the little grey Fergie,
Just to get back to the spanners and rags:
Just to climb up to the choke and the throttle –
In dirty old tee-shirt and oily blue bags.

Just to enjoy the sound of the engine,
'Miss' in a cylinder needing some care:
Just to show love by lifting the bonnet,
Unscrewing a sparkplug and finding a spare.

Then when it's purring to utter perfection,
Let up the clutch and engage the first gear:
I'm off on a joyride round the old dirt-track,
With cow-dung and mud right up to my ear.

Oh, those emotions that well in my spirit,
As fumes from the petrol freshen the air!
Oh, to go grandly around the old holding –
With little grey Fergie taking me there!

The cows and the sheep will look up and marvel,
Combustion like thunder spoiling their cud:
They'll say with delight, 'There's the fine fellow,
With a love of Tiree deep-dyed in his blood!'

PLOUGHING

That afternoon my father said,
'I'll drive the tractor,
You'll guide the plough.'

Ancient potatoes demanded
(Who would doubt it?)
The old-style single-furrow,
Devoid now of four-footed traction,
But chained to the Ferguson:
They'd refuse to grow
In hydraulic scrawl:
Traditional treatment,
Hands-on, or nothing.

Draw-chain tightening,
I gripped long iron handles,
Sinking share, levelling angle,
Anticipating sharp-edged furrow,
Turf turned immaculately,
End-to-end straightness,
Perfect depth.

But that old iron warrior
Of jealous rusting vintage
Refused to obey orders,
Would not lift its nose,
Or straighten the bottom plate:
It pulled over, upwards,
Then on its side, carrying me
Transversely, my arms straining,
My legs lurching, my feet knotting,

Zig-zagging, until finally
At the uneven furrow's end,
It swiped my ribs contemptuously
With those hard handles,
And flopped ironically
On the ground.

Seagulls cried overhead,
Whirled mockingly,
Squawking laughter.
The Ferguson trundled
Along regardless
For the next furrow,
While I mourned
The sure-footed
Friendly horse.

OLD ALBION BINDER

You were conceived in the era of the horse,
When a team hauled you heavily through corn,
But now, towed by grey Ferguson tractor,
You are empowered by a single beast:

Your broad platform and cutter bar
Slicing the standing grain, canvases
Rattling round and over runners,
Occasionally seeking adjustment,
Sending thousands of ear-heavy oat-stalks
Upwards on double elevator canvases
To be compacted into shapely sheaf,
By the impatient packer, ready
To land beside those muscular spikes,
While knotter twines a band
Round young yellow-green trunk:

Next sheaf comes, whacked downwards,
Applying pressure to release bar,
While these harsh mechanical arms
Give birth to ageless gentle Ceres,
Slim-waisted golden maiden,
Augmenting glorious display,
Stretching to field's perimeter.

HARNESSING TRACTORS

Fresh-born in death, Ceres stands,
Arrayed in primordial propriety,
Momentarily transfixed proudly,
As her deadly life-giver passes,
Huge central wheel powering all,
Drive-chains dripping oil on pulleys,
Clacking, crunching, whirring,
Revolving rake above the platform
Knocking the arrogant young corn
Backwards into razor-toothed blade,
Human grip adjusting height and depth
From that seat of power above
Noise-filled mechanism.

As you clatter inharmoniously onwards,
Slicing all bounteous fecundity,
She falls slowly facewards, sighing,
Resting weary travails on sharp stubble,
Until, raised by heaving hands,
She joins her entourage again
In stooks, row upon row,
Curving into the sunset
And the golden stackyard.

CROFTER ON A TRACTOR

You give ample warning of your approach,
Diesel combustion exploding in still morning
Of light mist, animals waiting for some silage
From big black puddings, richly scented:
High upon rubber rings of hard tread,
Sheltered in once-red, now-rusted metal,
You pass me with a heavy-handed wave,
Daring momentarily to take it off the wheel,
As your battle-scarred Massey-Ferguson
With its speed-lines of hardened cow-dung
Rattles rumbustiously to your destination:
You hook the bale, and heave it to the herd,
Lowing longingly for the noisy parousia
Of their earth-bound saviour,
King of a cantankerous croft.

SCHOLARS' CROFT

On this patch of ground we toil
Across the centuries of arid days,
Clearing rocks and stones and sticks,
Applying ploughshares to unyielding clays:
Sowing the seed, removing tangling weeds,
Frightening off the birds, the alien crows,
Maintaining fences, keeping out the foe,
Ensuring that the moisture softly seeps,
And that, in time, essential crops will grow.

At harvest, as the binder throws out sheaves,
And stooks appear across the stubbled fields,
As corn-stacks rise in rows within the yards,
And blistered hands secure the summer's yields,
They come, the inspectors of our ways:

They watch us idly from their roadside rest,
And pull out pen and paper as they gaze:
'Let's study them,' they say with lofty joy,
'That subaltern crew in our postcolonial ploy.'

OLD HAY-TURNER

Abandoned in a far corner
Of a far field, in a hollow
Beside a ditch, to die,
To disintegrate remote
From humans, rust to rust,
Your spokes still bristle
Above stubborn grass
Fighting to claim you,
Overgrown, stormed,
Scorched, lashed,
Yet defiant in death.

In this indifferent summer
Fifty years after disposal
You are still kicking up
A hard crop of thoughts
In all who care to look,
Reminding them that
Your abandoners
Have disappeared
From a changed croft
With no more hay.

My mental hayfield
Feels your sharp prongs
In its painful swathes
As you turn them
To harsh daylight
To ripen sorely.

A crow sits on your seat:
Beside your iron wheels
Withered irises proclaim
An unending elegy:
A way of life
Gone.

GRAVEYARDS

Crofters all have their own,
Those special plots where
Metal skeletons are committed
Rust to rust, to decay
In elemental dissolution
In a secluded hollow,
Reapers, tractors, trailers,
A plough or two, a hay-turner,
A road-wrecked van,
Ribs of iron rising red
Through burnished grass,
Thistles jagging the air,
Irises drooping yellow,
Nature labouring to recycle
Carefully collected clutter,
Taking its revenge
On this ironic lot,
Imposing last rites.

They resist strongly;
In pale moonlight,
A dance macabre
Of radius arms
Linked in chains,
Eyes hanging
Out of sockets,
Broken axles,
Tyreless wheels
Taking a final spin.

Implements reassemble
Their harrowing spectacle
As old headlamps
Gleam wickedly,
Cursing crofters.

ECHOES, IMAGES, VOICES

NO LEFT LUGGAGE

There is no Left Luggage in my island,
Nowhere to leave the memories,
The people, the animals, the implements,
The boats, the buildings, the tides,
The views across the Sound,
Ben More for ever leading my eyes,
The storms, the calms, the days
Between two elements, when skies hung
Menacingly over Coll, and we did not know
How tomorrow would be, or whether
The *Claymore* would manage a call.

There's nowhere to leave the voices,
The crofters chatting over the wall,
Or at the meeting of Ferguson tractors
In the middle of the road, blocking traffic;
The days at the sheep-dipping,
When laughter splashed through sodden wool,
Stories floated in the dip-rich air,
Niall Iain went deep-sea again, Iain Mòr
From Tòrr a' Bhaile chuckled as he pushed
The sheep's head below the oily surface,
And Calum Salum arrived with his thick glasses
To retard unnecessary progress.

There's nowhere to leave Neil Jackson's voice,
Chanting at Crossapol auction mart,
'A ten-pound bid, a ten-pound bid, who says
A ten-pound bid, at ten a bid, at eleven…
At twelve…at twelve…and it goes to Jim Henry.'
His stick clinches the sales of sheep and cows
To Lowland drovers with green expanses,
Their soft hats, grey raincoats over
Waterproof trousers, and Wellington boots.
We go for tea and sandwiches
In Paterson's barn, a straw-filled café,
Swept clean for the occasion,
With no cobbled cows;
Home we go with fat cheques
For the lean and hungry winter.

There's nowhere to leave an evening's fishing,
The sharp tug on the line,
The hard, expectant heave over the gunwale,
The long swathes of orange sunset
On blue-green water as we glide towards the buoyed anchor,
With glittering, flapping catch,
The dog swimming to meet us;
I still go searching for that boat,
The *Peace and Plenty* which eludes me,
Long since turned to dust above the shore,
As I try to translate memories into realities,
Make the experiences pulse again
Through flesh and blood.

There's nowhere to leave the Gaelic services;
Balemartine church with sharp, rigid pews
Is now closed, but still I hear
My father's rhythmic voice
In sermon and in prayer,
And Niall Ruadh leading the singing
Of trembling, rough-edged psalms,
Nasally pentatonic, vibrating,
Ebbing, flowing, swirling,
With a withering congregation;
My mental tapes are indelible.

Service ended, I open the church door,
And glimpse Ben More again, constant
Above the wave-tossed rocks.
It remains my eternal landmark.

There's just no escape from these cases,
Filled with albums, recordings, mementoes,
Recollections, sayings, comments,
Which weigh me down, the journey
Heavy sometimes.

I think of Johnny Pakistani –
Himself now part of my luggage –
Trundling uphill to Croish on his bicycle,
Grateful for the downhill ride to Caolas,
The wind on his back, feet at right angles,
That vast portmanteau on his handlebars,
His miraculous merchandise for sale,
Displayed on sooty floors.

Like him, I rearrange the contents,
Stopping to take fresh bearings
From that distant mountain, praying for strength,
As I step across the machair
Or down the Milton road,
Never knowing which package
I must open next, which tape will play.

Exhausted, I pause and think,
And then set off again
With my indispensable baggage,
Which I will never leave behind.
It helps to keep me going
As I head for the horizon.

CROSSAPOL AUCTIONEER

Neil Jackson's voice sings on,
The precentor of sale psalmody,
Giving out the line, minds following,
Wondering where the litany will stop:
'At fifty bid, at fifty bid, at fifty-two,
At fifty-two, at fifty-two…'
Donald Kennedy looks up briefly,
Tommy MacKinnon looks down,
John MacArthur smiles wryly:
I scan anxious faces, old friends
Wearing tense expressions,
Bonnets adjusted, foreheads scratched,
Cigarettes dangling on bottom lips:
'At fifty-two, at fifty-three, at four,
At four…At fifty-four pound a bid,
And it goes to Andrew Henry…'
The tension abates momentarily,
As a black stirk leaps out,
And a brown one (with white head) leaps in,
And the liturgy begins again…
'Who says sixty pounds? Sixty?
At sixty…At two, at three,
Sixty-three, at three a bid…'
Blue skies bend downwards
To kiss the corrugated iron roof,
Straggly wool flutters on fences,
Boots squelch, oilskins crinkle,
Taking no chances, wary in mud,
Easy to sink…'at seventy, at seventy,
At seventy bid, and it's all over
At seventy pound bid for 'um…

At seventy pound bid,
To Andrew Henry Number Two...'
The stick comes down.

Droves of drovers stand round the ring,
Leaning, relaxing, knowing their power,
As Alec Hector and John Lachie
Worry about the winter,
Seeing the green fields of Glenisla,
Beyond the barren rocks of Tiree,
The *Loch Carron* taking out cattle,
Bringing in bales of hay.

Aye, Neil Jackson rules the world
In that little booth in Crossapol,
Controls the future, designs destiny,
Precentor of Corson's market music,
Intermediary between poverty
And sufficiency, between buyers
And sellers, pushing price upwards,
Eye scanning distant minds,
His voice demanding attention,
Commanding all to listen and obey,
Or die. And I still hear him.
When will he ever stop?

LAST SAIL

That glorious evening comes to mind
When we sailed the *Shamrock* in the tranquil pool,
Up there in Bàgh, where the stream would wind
Its slow way down, flowing deep and full:

The sun sank westwards in a broadening trail
Across the wide Reef with radiant ray,
As my father, master supreme of well-trimmed sail,
Set that model yacht upon its way:

I see it yet, heeling in the evening breeze,
Beginning its voyage a hundred yards away,
Main sail filling, jib sails set at ease,
Stem slicing water in a sparkling spray.

I watched in wonder as *Shamrock* did his will,
Holding mid-channel in the final heat,
Then directly crowned his guiding skill
By making harbour at my waiting feet.

HAUNTED

I jumped with happy, joyful terror
The other evening in 'Coll View';
The garret, above those bare, white joists,
Burnt by the Tilley's friendly light,
Was alive with familiar trembling,
Creakings, groanings,
Bangs and wallops, flat things falling,
Face down, knocking others off their pedestal,
As if my father, preparing his Sunday sermons
In his favourite sanctuary, seriously writing,
Had dispatched a heavy tome, which had in turn
Collided with the old Singer sewing-machine,
Sending its reels and spindles
Bouncing off the pedals, flying along
The cold, shining, yellow-brown linoleum.
Theology had some very strange
Outworkings, miraculous effects,
Hard-hitting at times.

Was this a visitation, a revenant?
Could I perhaps glimpse the ectoplasm
Of that devoted man again, hear the voice,
See the sparkle of blue eyes.
The noise, in truth the music, was
So familiar that I lost fifty years
Of distance between now and then.

I crept out to the garret stairs,
Straight, steep, made for storms,
Rescued happily in the nick of time
From a wrecked ship, and put to use,
To convey the purposeful feet of
Human generations.
My eyes drilled the darkness,
Searchlights in the gloom.

She came down gently,
Tail in the air, a happy purr
Of recognition.

DARKROOM

'Let there be darkness,'
I said, closing the door,
Reverting to primordial
Principles of chaos,
Finding trays, chemicals,
Arranging processes
To bring my father's image
Into permanent life,
Wrinkles wrought on face,
Strong stubble slabbed
With Ferguson tractor oil
Fresh from sump,
Mild outline of smile
On firm flesh
Gentle with years
Of hardness,
Soft cloth bonnet
Billowing thoughtfully.

I marvel every moment
At the bright permanence
I created in that darkness.
That's my father still
Undimmed by time.

Today in the darkroom
Of my mind, I struggle
With unknown chemicals,
Watching, waiting
To see an image emerging,
A simile like silver
Running from the film,
A mercurial metaphor
Rising under ultra-violet
Perceptions, until I perceive
A picture faintly formed,
In there somewhere.

Let there be darkness
Until I fix permanently
This transient moment.

MY FATHER WINNOWING

A lean man
Standing straight
Above a slim slope
With a thin gradient
Slanting below him
Dusted with frail chaff
Redundant yellow husk
Forming a fragile triangle
On dry grass tips
Tapering southwards.

Gentle north wind
On sharp spring day
Powers his rhythm
Below a deep sky
Fan undulating
Lightly above his head
Such clean control
Of those flexing arms
In primordial dance
With unseen
Ceres.

Aerobics natural
To this lithe stalk
A well-winnowed
Sparing branch
Of essential
Goodness.

No wonder
His trim crop
Finely sown
Never went
To seed.

MAN OF STONE
Haugesund, Norway, 6 June 2015

Man of stone, my friend,
Weathered, moss-marked,
As natural as the rain,
The wind, the sun, the snow,
Made by sculptor's hand
Without any ornamentation,
Yet adorned by the elements,
You stand there with your cloth cap,
Contoured softly in solid stone,
Tangible, touching my heart,
Awakening deep kinship
With your resistant rock.

I recognise your kindly face
As my own flesh and blood:
You are my father's double,
With chiselled brow, high,
Storm-defying cheek-bones,
Exuding peace, unchanging,
Your lips pursed gently,
Your eyes searching my soul,
Their dark glimmer of light
Becoming a shaft of lineage.

Yes, you are the very image
Of my father, his identikit,
Hewn from the same stone,
From the same geology,
Cut to perfection by a master,
Fashioned to fight life's forces,
To throw loving endurance
In the face of adversity.

You are anonymous, my friend,
With nothing to disclose your name,
Destined to be forgotten
Except for those still close,
Still remembering in Haugesund,
Still able to place you
Within their biological strata.

Yet I know who you are,
And you will know who I am:
You have been waiting for me
To cross the ocean, to match you
To my own father, to see in you
His likeness, to recognise
The softness of solidity,
The solidity of softness,
The glorious morphology
Of ordinary, unassuming greatness,
Deepest, plainest, finest humanity
Framed eternally
In living stone.

MY FATHER AT THE ANVIL

Today I saw that miracle again
Through the smoke of time's smithy;
There you were, lifting the anvil
By its horn, high above your head,
Answering a neighbour's challenge,
Then lowering it gently on its base,
Not an ounce of unnecessary flesh
On your riveted iron skeleton,
With its softly solid bones;
Not a boastful, needless word,
Everything pared down with cutters
To the barest of essentials,
Hot from blazing bellows,
Cooled in sizzling water;
Every reluctant band of metal
Made to measure the hoof
Of every horse, hammered
Hard on that unwieldy anvil
Under your mighty muscles,
Controlled perfectly by
Those enormous hands
That gripped God's Word
In sparing eloquence
In a varnished pulpit
On Sabbath days,
Now moving mountains
Effortlessly, easily,
In life's workshop,
By an elevating power
Beyond human measure.

SAWING WOOD

'Such a mindless task!'
That's what I thought too,
Until in that old workshop
I plied the Bushman saw
Across the crumbling lengths
That I had stored for firewood.

Somehow they came to life,
A spark emerged with every cut,
An internal fire was kindled,
Deep within my being.
The rotting wood lived again,
As through experiences I travelled,
And while travelling looked around
That universe of creativity:

The anvils and the hammers,
The bolts, the clamps, the drills:
The planes, the dyes, the spanners,
The tools that nothing kills:

'We are still here,' they shouted,
'And now we want your mind:
Your father used us proudly,
And you are of his kind.
For too long we've been idle,
But we've bided well our time:
You come here and use us,
And knock sparks from ancient rime.'

Poetic they were indeed, versifying
Effortlessly from their perches,
The traces of rust, the cobwebs,
Lending colour to their iron words,
Eloquent, visionary facilitators
Of thought and action.

As I sawed on, looking, listening,
I noticed the boat of the future
Sitting quietly between me and the door,
Her planks shaped elegantly,
Steamed to perfection,
Held by those brass rivets on the bench,
Her gentle sheer rising proudly,
Her beam swelling on a strong shoulder,
Her bow slicing Gunna Sound,
Her sail filled on a morning breeze.

Fresh shavings covered my feet,
And not the sawdust from old wood:
Even the sea licked my boots,
And salt sharpened my lips.

Sawing wood – 'a mindless activity'?
Only if you haven't got
A mind.

ECHOES, IMAGES, VOICES

PUMP HOUSE

Today I break sticks
In this house of memories,
Axe falling heavy on battens,
Its head cracking glazing
Off the old sink.

Two sinks, in fact,
With a wringer bar between,
Where I turned a handle
On soap-sudded washdays,
Felt fresh wind blasting
Through open doors.

And down there the dairy
With red crocks, basins,
Milk being skimmed with
Corrugated scallop-shells,
Churn turning, turning,
Butter walloping,
Appearing yellow
When patted tastily
Between small fingers.

Above on the rafters,
Boyhood's fleet of puffers,
Fishing-boats, cargo-ships,
Built by a happy hand,
Lies stranded on a plank,
Awaiting the breaker's hammer
For fifty years.

As I break those sticks
For winter kindling,
Those boats remain:
I realise that I cannot
Break memories
Without breaking
My own heart.

THE OLD WELL

How often as a boy I primed the pump
With bucketfuls of water till it foamed
With refreshing surges from the rock below,
Essential for the lives of all we owned.
That clattering handle, high above my head,
Heaved down by little hands with trembling grasp,
And up again, to catch the freshest draught,
Still pumps within my mind, though years ago
We closed the ancestral well, with concrete slabs.

Its eighteen feet of depth defied the driest drought,
Its stonework holding strong throughout the years,
Becoming narrower or so it seemed, as I looked down
And saw my own reflection in its refreshing stream.
Part of me was nurtured deep within that soil,
Made and moulded by the mineral wealth
Of ancient seams integral to the earth.

But then water from the loch arrived,
And, tapping into the island's common source,
We closed our well – something 'better' came.
Yet, behind the Pump House, it now bides its time,
Ready to serve, when, weary of the standard flow,
We open it again, and find once more
The refreshment needed by our jaded soul.

NEW FIRE

Fifty years is a long time
To be without a fire
Where it ought to have been,
Burning, lighting, warming,
Drying, airing, soothing,
Comforting, giving the room
Gentle currents of cleansing,
Lifting spirits,
Sparking life.

The old hearth was dead,
Killed with hardboard facade,
And no longer did figures appear
In the embers, no longer did stories
Lick their way round the flames,
Kissing their lively shadows
On the cheeks of children.

Fashion's flat-lining, bland,
Deadly concealer of reality
Hid that theatre from view,
And dampness reigned
In curtains and furniture,
On walls and floors,
Overcoming electric optimism,
Hopelessly switch-controlled.

But now smoke rises again
From that well-nested chimney
Clean-swept in readiness,
And the ceilidh returns:
Walls sing quietly,
Tables tell stories,
Hands stretch out,
Cats curl cautiously,
Marvelling that winter
No longer rules with
Icicles on its claws.

OLD RUGGED CROSS

A warm Sunday afternoon
In Aunt Annabel's best room
In the cottage by the shore,
Dust dancing in a sunbeam
As two china dogs listened
Each side of the fireplace
To Sydney MacEwan singing
'The Old Rugged Cross';

I was far away on a hill
On the bumpy velvet couch
Laying down my trophies
When I noticed the slowing
Of the wobbling turntable,
Its heavy-headed needle
Scratching the pitted wax,
The singer finally growling
The last words, eating
Them like soft bones
In a dying drawl –

The two wally dugs
Smiling with delight
As they recognised
Their master's voice
In that crocheted room
Of damply sweet tones

Replayed this very minute
From a scratched disc
On a gramophone
Which I cannot now
Rewind until I find
The handle.

MOON LANDING, JULY 1969

My ear set furtively to the quiet radio
Picked up that 'one small step for man'
In Neil Armstrong's quavering voice,
As I marvelled ponderously off-stage,
Pouring painful cups of heavy tea,
While in the shadowed living-room
Friends with hushed condolences
Mourned the departure of Annabel,
Lifeless in a Glasgow mortuary,
Last of the 'Coll View' MacDonalds.

That explorer extraordinary
Commuted across the Atlantic
In tall-stacked steamships
Between Liverpool and Montreal,
On snaking, twisting trains
Between Winnipeg and Vancouver,
Her steps, however small,
Seldom faltering until now,
Walking Manitoba's prairies,
Seattle's store-lined streets,
Tiree's moonlit machairs.

'One giant leap for mankind'
From Tiree to the Sea of Tranquillity,
But that shadow still hovered over earth,
Enfolding those who saw no new thing
In the frail human planet as perceived
From famous footsteps on the moon.

ROADS OF MEMORY

ROAD HOME

That road I walk today
In sunshine, wind and rain,
While sitting miles away;
My restless heart and brain

Seeing familiar tracks
With a central path of grass,
Where horses and their carts
Would regularly pass.

Trudging to that school,
In a morning of dark cloud,
Grit invading shoes;
I dread the daily round

Of drill and shouting,
Belt poised to warm small hands;
No talking! Stop the noise,
And listen to commands!

But then the slow cloud clears,
Time's passage frees the skies:
I walk homewards, bright
Among flowers, and grass, and cries

Of birds on moors, and lark
Soaring high in song;
The Caolas march I see;
The last stretch will not be long.

Gunna's roughness is unmoved,
It still defines the Sound,
Hard shapes of Coll and Mull,
Eternal, changeless ground.

Gently down from Croish,
The slope conveys me fast;
I climb the old back wall,
Another school day past.

But now the years have run,
As that last stretch I walk;
The school has long since closed,
And dead friends cannot talk.

SINGLE TRACK

You are the queen of roads
In your singularity of purpose,
Your stripped-down essentials,
Nothing to spare for frivolity:
You demand attention
From alert wayfarers,
Divert the dozing
Towards predetermined ditches,
Inculcate discipline,
Impose rules of courtesy,
Preferring to line your pockets
With safe tolls from
Appreciative travellers.

You are pocked with potholes,
Sinking verges to catch the careless,
Grass sprouting from your centre,
Irregular chunks of turgid tarmac,
Gravel edges to graze bicycles,
Give their owners your special
Roller-coaster rides
Into reality.

You specialise in bends
Crawling quietly over hills,
Blind only to those
Who know no contours
Beyond their own flat minds,
Producing sharp surprises
To hone our intellects,
To promote gentle, gracious,
Sure-handed salutations.

Far from you the turmoil
Of the stressful motorway,
Thoughtless thundering
At death-dealing speeds:
You belong to another era,
Another time, another place,
When carts clattered clumsily
On their purposeful pottering
Behind horses' tails,
When reins held heads high:
You hold to your unbending
Irregular rules, regardless of
Modernity's world:
We must yield to you.

Obeying your commands,
Learning our lessons,
We see the world well,
Admire the vistas,
Soaring skies,
Sweeping bays,
Absorb beauty slowly.

Thanks to you, single track,
We learn to live and move
And have our being.

ROAD TO DAMASCUS?

No, it was only the road to Caolas,
A wee road to a wee place
Of no earthly significance:
A road not taken by the great
Or the good, only by crofters
Clomping along on foot alone
Or with their lumbering carts,
To or from Ruaig or Salum
Or Gott or Scarinish.
Are these names on the atlas
Of the world? Who cares?

Strange to think that my father
Was walking along that road
One night, just going home,
And God – yes, God –
Spoke to him.
God knew that track
And that man.

No flash of light,
No great event
Making headlines,
No false feeling.

He walked onwards,
That preacher man,
Quietly, gently,
Telling the story
In Gaelic and English,
Until one day
God met him again
And took him
Along the road
Home to Himself.

SHORE LINES

Lights And Storms

HYNISH

Here in the afternoon,
Dull with cloud and close rain,
The world becomes radiant;
The hill wears a crown of silver,
Road ribboned in celestial wonder;
A wave breaks as I walk upwards
Through the heavy turf.

The sharp, grey granite speaks
Of genius, of craftsmen's hands
Holding chisels and refining millimetres
To achieve perfection, twice building,
First on land, and then on treacherous rock
That eternal tower, pin-point sharp
Against halo-blaze of orange
Sunset.

This is another world, another time
When building was sacrificial,
When lives were laid down in granite
As foundations for others' futures,
When Alan Stevenson lay in the barrack
Thirteen miles from health and safety,
Rejoiced in danger and defiance,
Thrown around by thunderous power,
Held his Bible hard to his eyes,
And prayed that God would grant him
The salvation of sailors.

The *Pharos*, ancient light enshrined
In modern miracles of technology,
Sends off her red bird, seeking a place
To perch on that torrent, descending
Safely on Skerryvore,
And back she comes, dove-like
With a message.

The lights of workers' houses
Flash through the gathering dusk,
The tower stands sentinel,
Stark chimneys pierce the sky,
Reflecting the shafts
Of sunset's greater beacon.
Sea laps round
The shining pier.

This place is radiant.
This place is sacred.

HYNISH DAM

That dam in Hynish has power
Far beyond the knowing
Of Alan Stevenson,
The day he stopped the waters,
Built a conduit, and harnessed them
To clean that dock.

But he saw the deep essentials,
Power within simplicities,
Appropriately channelled,
Given focus, control,
Purpose.

A greater vision flowed
When sluices were opened,
As the lade whirled down,
Scouring out the sand
To keep the dock clear
And maintain the light
Shining brightly
On Skerryvore.

SKERRYVORE

Although you are the fairest
Of all the deep-sea lights,
And though we see you flashing
Throughout the darkest nights,
I've never sung a 'Thank you'
Or given you some praise
For all the ships you've guided
With your far-reaching rays.

You stand firm upon the granite
That's solid in its grain,
That will not move in tempest
Or shudder in a gale:
And you yourself are granite,
Cut out by sharpest blade,
Tiree is your foundation,
Of Mull your core is made.

You fill my mind with wonder,
As you stand above the shoals,
A monument to greatness
And engineering goals:
The Stevensons have made you
Their own immortal sign,
But you have also made them
The greatest of their line.

The mariner who's sailing
To the west of far Tiree
Will see your tower rising
Above the wildest sea:
Your lantern crowns your courses,
Caps rows of curving stone,
And flashes out its warnings
With timings of its own.

In a world of storm and trouble,
As oceans roar and foam,
You stand out there regardless,
To guide each sailor home:
And in an age of wreckers,
You state with certain tone
That every life is precious,
Each sinew and each bone.

I look across and marvel
As I see you like a pin
Upon the far horizon
As the night is closing in:
And as the darkness settles,
And your beam lights up the sky,
I bless the men who built you –
Their name will never die.

RED FALCON

In memory of the Fleetwood trawler *Red Falcon* wrecked off Skerryvore with all hands on 15 December 1959. Our Tiree Christmas party was held on the evening on which the tragedy was confirmed.

Your sinking has not sunk
From my childhood memory:
I see you still, battling storms,
West of the huge wave-sweeps
Of Skerryvore, as the flashes
Tell you to keep clear of danger,
But you cannot do so, unable
To turn or steer or stop,
The brutal south-westerly
Whipping you on to a lee shore,
Pounding you, smashing you,
Tearing you apart on boiling reefs,
Hurling your crew into the sea,
Showing no mercy.

The great lighthouse warned you well,
But a warning cannot stop
Nature's force, no power surpasses
The hidden unknown energies
Of unfathomable oceans.
What's a ship to them?

Fleetwood in sadness,
Fragments of its Christmas
Coming ashore unknown
On Tiree sands.
Children weeping
With empty hearts.

Santa's gift trembled
In my hands that night,
The red wrappers somehow
Bringing the *Red Falcon*
To my mind, fixing it eternally –
A bird that did not find
Its family nest,
A boat that did not find
Its safe haven.
It gives me still
No peace.

MALIN

That name haunts my weather;
I feel it in my anticyclones of hope
When there has been rain in past hour,
The wind backing northerly, good,
And in my depressions, filling,
Expected soon, wind cyclonic
Veering westerly, Force 9 to Storm 10,
Showers later. Visibility poor.

I malinger in my mind,
Listening intently to broadcasts
Of meteorological profundities
Reduced to simple breezes,
Normalising life's isobars,
Internalising data, seeing
My own calms, my turmoils,
Through objective forecasts:

As I feel those words of weather
Playing deep in my soul's seas,
Contextualising my personal island,
I know who I really am –
A man from Malin.

STORM NOTES
14 December 2013

The old house becomes orchestral,
A cacophony of blustering music.

Walls with peaked gables provide
Woodwind instruments of all kinds,
Wooden doors on their last stands
Bend inwards on their hinges,
Whistling strange, novel tunes,
Windows groan and grind,
Foundations reel in pain
As external objects collide callously,
With punishing percussion,
The cat-flap clicks and clanks,
No harmony here at ground level,
Stiff resistance, hit or miss.

But skywards we have
Purposeful, powerful playing
With dynamic deflections
Of moving air, pressure held
Momentarily, venting upwards,
Gutters are chanters
As the bag of wind blasts
Through pipes,
Chimney-heads and pots
Are drones,
Slates play drums.

The well-nailed ridge
Conducts cleverly,
Knows the score,
Has read it many times,
Holds the musicians together,
Proud Pipe Major.

The top storey dances,
Merry in the storm.

BACK DOOR MUSIC

That old back door in 'Coll View' –
How I miss its stormy orchestration!
Wood-wind instruments from the south-west
Gave it the haunting high tones,
While the cello and the bass came thundering
With the heavy showers,
Violin parts, l'allegro, il pensoroso,
It did the lot without a conductor –
And that unforgettable mouth-organ
With its doleful Highland waltzes
At the very threshold where it had rotted
Gently in the perpetual rain.

It resonated, harmonised, modulated,
Gave the boot-dirtied runners the proms,
With a fluid outflow of limpid drops
Of deep emotion to round off the concert.

My musical soul is much the poorer
Since a wind-proof door killed
All players.

There are more ways than one
Of murdering a tune.

STRONG WINDS

Strong winds blow in Scotland,
Compass-defying brutes that swell
Unexpectedly to test your loyalty;
Just try an island, flat, sandy,
Four thousand feet below Ben Nevis,
Where you would be a fool to relax,
Talk breezy nonsense about beauty,
About long, languid summer days:

Because that's not the island,
Nor is it Scotland of uplands
And lowlands, and funnelling glens.

Instead of blethering, test your feet,
Their ability to hold on when storms
Rage out of nowhere, intent on murder,
And whip your body into shreds
That your mind cannot comprehend.

You see, it's easy to babble in calms,
To talk with knowledgeable ignorance
Of loveliness in the sheltered dream,
But try standing on yon headland in Force
Ten that comes out of everywhere:

It's grip you need, toes like hooks,
Right into that ancient gneiss:
The ability to hang in there
When nothing else holds.

LIGHTS AND STORMS

POWER CUT

A weather bomb struck this morning
At 06.30 hours, exploding thunderously,
Lightning compacted into a fireball,
Illuminating the township, but snuffing out
All human lights. Stair-light dead,
I descended gingerly, feeling each step,
My limp hand trying to read braille
In natural contours, banisters, skirting,
My toes detecting tipping-points,
Until they found terra firma
On creaking floor-planks.

Darkness ruled, as I crawled
To the living-room, lit three candles
With torchlight on the mantelpiece,
And then bowed low in trembling hope
That last night's embers might still have life.

The Vestal Virgins had performed well,
Protecting the sacred flame, as I prayed
For its speedy resurrection, aided by
Rolled pages from *The Herald* –
No angel by daylight, certainly,
Or during the reign of electricity,
But surprisingly merciful
In my deep, dark gloom.

Lightning illuminated explosively
My electro-dependency syndrome,
My terror at such a grim prospect
As living one hour by candlelight,
My fear of having to boil water
In a small, smoky fire-blackened pot,
In radiant, once-friendly flames.

As I knelt abjectly before that trinity,
Beseeching them for a speedy reconnection
To the Great Grid of our Salvation,
I heard distinctly the ghosts of relatives
Long gone, but ever present,
Laughing irreverently.

BINS AT WAR

Across the grass their innards pour
Detritus of human consumption,
Empty tins that once protected meat,
Bullet-proof packaging to kill bacteria,
Paper to feed propaganda to news-starved minds:
Plastic tanks to aid domestic inadequacy
Now themselves prove inadequate,
As they fall dead before the barrage,
Struck down behind embankments,
Green, blue, black infantrymen,
Laid low, their lids wide open,
Requiring to be closed by human hand,
As blasts from the sky strike hard,
And blinds are drawn down
To shut out the grim reality.

Aye, it's like the Somme here today,
In ways that carry a disposable truth:
These bins were sent to their deaths
By mindless planners who did not know
The needs of remote Hebridean trenches.
One size fitted all, the one way to conquer
Enemies subtler far than those stiff soldiers.

If you lose one, there's a gap, of course,
But they'll send another and another
From their never-ending store,
Their wheels ready to squelch
Across the sodden ground,
Set up to fall to the hard hail
Of elemental forces, and then
Disappear in dead man's dump.

Bins lay down their lives
In the noble cause of rubbish,
Mingling themselves with mud,
Rain and hail, as merciless wind
Drives them hither and yon
Despite our best endeavours
To keep their lids on,
To make them stand proudly,
Put their heads above the parapet
For Queen and country again.

Mainland High Command is proud
Of its brave service bintalions.
But clerks in offices don't care:
They are obeying orders:
They are not their bins:
They are only chattels,
To be distributed as required
To keep other enemies at bay –
For the time being,
Until the next storm.

STORM

Yesterday I was fighting for life,
Pinned hard against a rock
On my own mental shoreline,
As the rogue-wave thundered in,
A torrent of words, foaming,
Furious, flailing, flashing,
Full of debris, gathered along
A multiplicity of seaways
Unknown to me, hurled
Hard at me, no escape,
No means to respond,
Clinging with fingernails
To cracks in ancient strata,
Enough to hold me
Till it ended
As usual.

I said nothing, no space,
No place, silence enforced,
Seaweed wrapped round my jaws,
My mouth stilled, as I struggled
Choking to rebuke
Wind and waves
With my local
Littleness.
Today I feel my bruises,
Check the damage.

Another cyclone gone,
Another storm.
We will weather
Waves of alien words.
We're only islanders,
Natives.

GROCERIES AND GOODS

CALUM SALUM'S SHOP

The Two Ronnies couldn't act it, it would be too hard for them –
Calum's grand emporium was Tiree's most splendid gem:
In that shack he carried all you'd need from stern to stem:
For your stays or drawers, he'd have thread to make a hem.

Calor Gas in cylinders would be lying at the door,
With pipes and tubes and bicycles, and wheels and spares galore:
Blowlamps and tobacco, spanners, hammers and much more –
No hardware merchant on this earth ever owned a better store.

There were ladders tied to rafters and rylock on the floor,
Many potential booby-traps, and unsteady folk who swore,
As hay-rakes fell, and planks of wood, most often three or four –
But Calum Salum hadn't heard of the Health and Safety bore.

Liquorice and gobstobbers, and chocolate in fat bars,
Maltesers, Aero, Five Boys, Turkish Delight and Mars,
Marshmallows, Wagon Wheels, and toffees in bright jars –
Calum Salum's deli made your belly reach the stars!

Asprin, Aspro, Askit, just in case your head was sore,
Sedatives and laxatives, he had them by the score:
These mixtures were most powerful, with delirium at their core,
But an even stronger remedy lay in glass towards the shore.

Aye, Calum was unflappable, with a pencil at his ear:
He'd take your list and look at it, and say, 'I greatly fear,
I do not have the Scrapex or the Veet or Iron Beer,
But, chust you wait a minute now, I'll have much better here!

'As I'm the "Cheneral Merchant", things "cheneral" you'll see,
But I also have specifics that are specific to Tiree:
I brew my own behind the rocks, the good old barley bree,
But keep it quiet, a charaid, because my licence is QT!'

From a needle to an anchor, from the cradle to the bier,
Calum Salum had it, and its lack you'd never fear:
Stock conrol was absent, but his shop was full of cheer –
His stock controlled our Calum, and a solution aye was near.

VAN DAYS IN TIREE

No supermarkets in the island
In the days when I was young,
But well-stocked vans provided
Enough to whet my tongue.

Archie came on Saturdays,
Good MacIntyre from Gott,
And his wheeled emporium
Had the bacon that we bought.

A Mars Bar was for Sunday
Though never sweet enough;
Sugar Puffs instead of porridge
Gave me some pleasant puff.

Archie was aye smiling,
A warm heart in his ways;
His mother was the storekeeper
In calm and stormy days.

On Thursdays it was Brown's van
With comics near the till –
The *Rover*'s great adventures
Gave my wee heart a thrill.

It brought me sherbet lollies
And fine Creamola Foam,
And liquorice like rulers,
All sorts to lick at home.

Harry Rutter was a winner
With the ladies in his van;
They rushed outside whenever
They saw that charming man!

And then upon a Wednesday,
We had a visit from the Co,
With Neil MacNeill from Scarinish
And his pencil out on show;

He held it on his ear-top,
Just like a cigarette,
And pulled it down directly
To scribble what you'd get.

He used a paper pokey
To record the growing cost,
With a line below the tally –
And not a penny lost!

Then we had the butcher
With his lovely mobile shop,
To sell us finest silverside
And often a good chop.

Donald came from Scarinish
With all the grandest cuts,
Gave you his star treatment –
The finest bullock butts!

Now as I head for Scarinish
When my supplies run low,
I think of the convenience
Of those days of long ago!

CO-OP-TED

From the lone Co-op on the low-lying island,
We buy our spuds and our tins of peas,
Our warm-up meals, our cakes and biscuits,
Our milk and veg, and packs of cheese.

We buy the six-packs and the brimming bottles,
And dream of evenings when we take our ease,
With Tunnock's tea-cakes and caramel wafers,
And a couple of flapjacks by our TVs.

That puts the crown on the eggs and bacon,
The rich brown chips with their drips of grease,
To hold our cholesterol at just the level
To clog our heart-valves the way we please.

As I wheel the trolley I feel I'm slacking,
As it gets heavier with every wheeze;
I'm just so grateful the boot is massive,
To take my loot in no small degrees.

I can't imagine how my ancient forebears
Could live on porridge, with no deep-freeze,
With no Co-op, no plastic wrappers,
No beef stroganoff, and no UHTs.

As I drive back to my home in Caolas,
My shopping's safe, though it's quite a squeeze;
My girth's increasing and my belt is bursting,
But I'll bless the Co-op for my cream teas.

GROCERIES AND GOODS

CATCHING
THE BOAT

DUNARA CASTLE

When do ships die? Do they enter
Other levels of life, brain, memory,
Blood, heart, emotions, perceptions?
Do they ever leave these deeper seas,
Visiting us eternally, a *Flying Dutchman*
Constantly on the fringe of ghostly dream?

My physical eyes never saw the 'Dunara',
But somehow she navigates inside me,
Through my people's smouldering affection
For her blazing furnace, her thick smoke,
Her brutal green rolling on blue Mulls as she hauled
Shy Hebrideans and loud Lowlanders to destinies
Beyond our knowing. And she's still there,
Heaving, controlling my similitudes,
Giving me comparisons as I light the fire –
'This is just like the "Dunara"' – and when I hear
A whistle piercing my ears, I think of that horn,
Summoning islanders to do homage to her iron
Rivets, her essential, indispensable bridging
Of worlds within, without, beyond, desired,
Forsaken…

She's anchored still, an enduring stac
In Village Bay, bringing the outside in,
Taking the inside out of that community,
Blowing her last St Kilda sound in 1930
To lift life away: sheep, shepherds,
Leaving an archipelago in her wake…

Sailing into memory, their memory,
My memory, with her straight sheer,
Sky-scraping masts, towering funnel,
Canvas dodgers, global storm-swept wheel
Steering her to worlds infinitely beyond
The ken of Martin Orme,
Launching her forged angularities
Down the slipway in Port Glasgow
One hundred and forty years ago.

The ship that shaped Hebridean
History, haunting me still
And forever, the immortal
Deathless 'Dunara'.

THE LOVELY OLD *CLAYMORE*

When I was a wee laddie, I'd leave my island shore
On the finest MacBrayne liner, the lovely old *Claymore*,
On a voyage bound for Oban with other calls in store –
I still feel great vibrations from the wonderful *Claymore*!

We drove along to Scarinish in our very finest gear,
As that mighty MacBrayne liner manoeuvred at the pier:
We were there and waiting when the ropes were thrown clear,
And delightful smoke was blasted from the lum of yon old dear.

Her funnel was the largest that I've seen upon the brine;
It was high and red and rounded, with a black top and a shine:
On her bow she had an image, a Highlander most fine,
With kilt and targe and toorie, and a claymore as a sign.

Captain John, he was her Master, a doughty man from Vaul;
He loved to make us welcome, with a chat for one and all:
His laughter rang like thunder through each dividing wall,
And the brand of his tobacco was the fragrant Bogie Roll.

When he would ring the telegraph, the ship would leap away,
And soon she would be surging through the breakers of Gott Bay,
Across to Arinagour, the first challenge of the day –
To meet yon wee red ferry that would often go astray.

Captain John would shout to them, as they went round and round,
'Just drop your hook, you Collaich, in case you'll all be drowned!'
He'd then call down the voicepipe, and the Chief, he never frowned –
They nudged the *Claymore* forward till the little boat was found.

When the derrick had stopped swinging, and the ferry sailed away,
We'd head towards the Cailleach through clouds of mist and spray:
The *Claymore* would be rolling, but fine food was on the tray –
The fattest Loch Fyne kippers that I've seen in all my day.

In Tobermory's sheltered harbour, the crew would take a nip
Through the back door of the Mishnish, and then rejoin the ship:
Two hours behind her schedule, she would resume her trip,
With vibrations that were terrible, and no chance of any sleep.

Then we'd head for Oban with the seagulls flying high,
And giving some deliveries to tourists from the sky:
The Sound of Mull was glorious, a hundred ships went by –
I'd steer the *Claymore* past them under Angus's careful eye!

When the 'Seaforth', that old banger, went down at Tiree pier,
The *Claymore* returned in grandeur to take away our fear:
She had her days of glory, and in Greece she'd soon appear,
Rebuilt to give the tourists some 'Hydra'-hodra cheer!

Oban Bay is terrible without the grand *Claymore*:
There's nothing there but ferries, and they are such a bore:
Each one is just a shoebox, with no surprise in store –
They're very drab successors to the colourful *Claymore*.

Since I have passed my sixty years and just a little more,
I love to walk in memory down by the Caolas shore:
I think I see that funnel, and I hear the engines' roar –
Oh, I've never seen the equal of the lovely old *Claymore*!

CATCHING THE BOAT

TAKING THE FERRY

I take the ferry everywhere
On my mind's ocean,
Set the gyro-compass
With no deviation from myself,
Autopilot firm with no concession
To manual, all controls to automatic;
She travels within my world,
Built to my own design,
Built by me, no other,
Crewed and captained,
Freighted and trimmed
Only by myself;

Schedules synchronised,
Together we depart
Constantly on time
To every unknown port;
Until I realise there is
No leaving of any harbour
Without this dreaded ferry
Taking her passage
Within this passenger;

And when I arrive, there is
No linkspan of thought
Where I do not see
That I have taken this ferry
To everywhere; yet
She berths ahead of me
Always, and never
Lets me leave
Without her.

Taking the ferry
Is no empty
Cliché;
It is a full
Sentence.

THE MIGHTY *CLANSMAN*

Press on, press on for Barra,
I hear the *Clansman* say,
As she powers through the channel,
Gunna Sound beneath her sway;
Her bone is in her molars,
And she's throwing out the spray;
Her bow-wave makes the yachtsmen
Get on their knees to pray.

Barratlantic's on the main deck,
And Brogan's fuel for cars;
There's bread to keep folk chewing,
And whisky for their bars;
Deliveries from Oban,
Derek Wilson's stacked with jars,
And Jewson's heaving timber
For another house's spars.

Press on, press on for Barra,
Till Maol Dòmhnaich comes to view,
But throttle back a little,
Till we align a buoy or two.
Thank goodness for the markers
As we make our passage through;
We'll swing by Kismul Castle,
And engage the thrusters too.

We'll use our Becker rudders –
Captain Norman has a way
Of steering to perfection
In every kind of bay;

He'll bring us in so gently
That the ancients all will say,
'There's skill in these new ferries,
Though I'd like the old to stay!'

Press on, press on for Barra;
Angus Brendan is on board,
And he's watching out for slackness
In the way we shift our load;
But the Big House down in England
With yon unruly horde
Will not despise the *Clansman* –
She knows how to use her sword!

FERRY STRANGE

How strange that no-one notices
The day the ferry comes;
When she is waiting at the pier,
There are no pipes and drums:

No welcome that will say to her,
'Well done, you faithful ship;
We want to thank you for your work,
And every perfect trip.

'We hardly see you as you cross
From Coll to our fine pier;
We take you all for granted,
And we never, ever cheer.'

But when our terrible ferry
Fails to tie the rope,
Struggles with the nasty swells,
And there is just no hope;

Well, then we'll surely make a noise,
And shout about our plight:
'She's just a tub, a wretched boat,
Her course was never right.

'Her Skipper doesn't know the way
To steer his awful boat;
I'd do far better there masel' –
He's just not worth a groat!

'In olden days when we were young,
The good ship aye came in;
Storm Force 12 was just a breeze
To the *Claymore* and her kin:

'We never lacked a single day
Without our lovely ship,
But now these awful ferries –
They give us all the pip!'

No, we never lacked a single day,
For it often was a week –
We did not see the ship at all,
But we could plug that leak.

With rolled-up sleeves we baked the bread,
And lived on oat-meal puds,
But now the Co-op is our life –
Its groceries and goods.

And we're the bosses, aye, 'tis us,
And the Captain – he's a dud!
If he misses just one day,
We'll have to chew our cud!

So let's be grateful, island folk,
And stop the girns and groans,
And just say 'Thanks, you faithful ship,
You're worth far more than moans!'

CATCHING THE BOAT

BODY IMAGE

'Why did they make me like this?'
The *Clansman* cries in despair:
'I don't like my blunt bow-visor,
And my stern is terribly square.

'I'm far too broad on the beam,
And I'm mocked in a sideways sea:
The waves at Lismore are bullies,
The current causes list to my lee:

'I'm far too high in the water,
My sides are just slabs, I am told,
And when I turn to the linkspan,
I look like a tank that's too old.

'My funnel resembles red Lego,
With black stuck over the top:
I hate that mast they've put on it –
Some day my patience will pop.

'Yon architect surely was silly,
He hadn't a clue about style:
He designed a tub to heave lorries –
He made me a hull of a pile!

'I hope there's a Doc at the Garvel
Who'll shortly take me in hand:
My calling is that of a speed-boat,
My vibes are really quite grand.

'I want to go shooting past Gunna
At forty-five knots and more;
I want a fabulous welcome
From spectators lining the shore.

'But what would they do without me?
Perhaps this is how I should be!
So I hope you will enjoy your journey
As I batter my way to Tiree!'

CATCHING THE BOAT

TIREE PIER

Hard-cored concrete roadway
Ending in a T-junction connects
With a highway unlimited,
But I cannot yet go beyond
The pierhead as I gaze now
Across Gott Bay, silver-edged
With wind-powered rainbows
High aloft, Kirkapol before me,
The Lodge, the graveyard.

Yet this is no dead end:
My ear hears welcomes,
My eye sees handshakes, hugs,
Painful partings, farewells,
Boats berthing bumpily
Against pitiless piles.

Ships braved battles here
On unyielding mornings,
Claymore struggling
Stern to pier end, desperately
Hanging on to mooring-ropes,
Creaking, squeaking, breaking,
Capstans hauling, heaving,
White-bonneted sailors
Hefting hawsers,
Captain shouting
To extinguish lights,
Pure darkness needed.

Aye, comings, goings,
Pipe-bands, funerals,
Triumphs, failures,
Cattle being whacked,
Glasgow Fair folk, school pupils,
Visitors, crofters, animals, vehicles,
Travelling this umbilical route.

Today Ben More is capped white,
Black-red ferry fuming forward,
Foaming frettingly into Gott Bay,
Listing lurchingly round,
Mating with the linkspan, churning
Her aggressively scheduled wake,
Stern-on.

Freight first, commercials,
Trundling trucks, hayloads,
MacKinnon, MacLennan,
Holding an island's destiny,
Articulating necessities:
Vans, cars, pedestrians.

I fill my Boarding Card among
Large striped women, swaggering surfers,
Bragging their macho boards and four-by-fours.

Driving down, I feel cold,
Fifty years passing instantly
Over a rusty green ramp.

CATCHING THE BOAT

Kirkapol shrinks now:
Graveyard buried
In deep distances.

PASSING ISLAND

(In appreciation of Professor Donald MacAulay.)

That island drifts away,
Sliding astern as I remain
Fixed on this moving ferry,
No part of me de-parting,
Remaining integrated,
My world going with me.

I watch the island
Passing passively,
Dropping into the sea
Rock by rock, hill by hill,
Shore by shore until
Finally it disappears
Into non-existence
Below eye's horizon.

Then in reflection
It comes up again,
Visible once more,
Never ever vanishing
From mind's refraction,
Its silhouette razor-sharp,
Shorelines dangerous,
Self now disintegrating
Into greater fragments
On the familiarly alien
Rocks of this
Passing
Permanent
Destructive
Creative
I-land.

SHORE LINES

VISION ON
THE LINE

LAZY EYE

Thank God that He made me
With that lazy eye, lethargic,
Slower than all the other eyes
Around me.

He knew how to extend my vision,
See wonders otherwise unseen,
Broaden my childhood perspectives
Beyond islands.

He knew how to steer my course
Through uncharted seas of mind,
Make me navigate carefully
Through wide channels.

That blemish opened great vistas,
Light flowing from life's spectrum,
To be processed in unhurried style
Of deeper meanings.

There are misprints on my pages
Because I could never focus on nearness:
Those distant beams ever lured me –
The archetypal lazy I.

OBAN STATION

Down the gangway I come, fifty-plus years ago,
Below the towering funnel of the old *Claymore*,
Say 'Goodbye' to Second Mate Archie at the gangway,
And wave to the duffle-coated Captain on the bridge,
My little feet stumbling on the foot-bars, my case heavy
With expectation, as they find their way on slippery
Pier-planks, with gaps to show the sea I've crossed.
Such an adventure! But it's not over yet,
As I pass the smiling porters with their green barrows,
And gain the concourse of that inviting station,
Sunlight glinting through glass, warming plants,
With an air of purpose and a hiss of steam.

There's grandeur here beyond my island knowing,
A sense of direction, a kind benevolence,
As I see the bookstall's wares, glimpse illustrations,
And notice these beguiling models of the ships
That make me proud. I've sailed on them with heroes,
Sea-dogs, and so I must spend my pocket-money,
So surely saved for such a day. I buy the *Claymore*,
And admire her for ever, playing on every window-sill
In that train carriage, pretending I'm the Captain.
That train too, its 'Black Five' wafting smoke,
I buy in miniature, coach by coach,
Retrospective and prospective moments
Linked together like these old LMS carriages,
As the clanging till swallows my pennies.

VISION ON THE LINE

Barrows clatter, rumble over the platforms,
Handles thrown back, as they stop, and parcels
Are heaved into the Guard's Van, where I see
A brake-wheel, and long to turn it, as if I had power.
And there's that Ballachulish tank, a MacIntosh,
Old as the misty hills, ancient as the twisting valleys,
But still going strong, its chimney
Straight and tall as a factory lum,
Crusted with hard, sweet, beautiful grime.
It's moving…Oh, it's not, but we are,
In a glorious illusion of relativity.
What wonders lie ahead!

Today, I still go down those long, leisurely platforms,
Hear birds chirping, and sniff the coal-whiffed air,
The warming dampness of the friendly steam.
But only as I dream, and play with those
Plaster-of-Paris models, as enduring
As that Ballachulish tank.

On this day in 2014, I groan among the customers,
Shut behind a grating, unable to move,
Caged in this confined entrapment,
Wondering, waiting, having bought nothing
But a tasteless sandwich and a dreary newspaper
In that apologetic booth with Oasis for comfort,
When those growling, tedious diesel units,
Kill my remaining energy.

Shore Lines

The warder has now turned
The lock, and I have been released
To face the cattle-truck
To Glasgow.

OBAN TO BUCHANAN STREET

Contending with the gradient that rises out of Oban,
Two grubby old 'Black Fives' are gradually slowing;
Sparks come out each chimney, grit is hitting noses,
Firemen hard are shovelling, the furnaces are glowing:

'The summit may be possible, if we keep on going,
Though I think we're puffing, peching, panting, groaning,
But at last we've made it, with whistle hoarsely blowing:
Then it's down to Connel with a rattle on each bogey:
Dalmally, flat to Tyndrum, Crianlarich then some snoring
To Killin, it's fairly level, with no gradients to slow us:
Buchanan Street, Buchanan Street, we'll reach you in the gloaming,
If we can keep up pressure at Lochearnhead and Glen Ogle,
With so many in these carriages, and goods so tightly loaded:
Balquhidder, on to Callander, and Doune with castle noble:
Stirling we'll stop at briefly, but keep the rhythm flowing:
At Cowlairs we'll see some sidings and trucks at our disposal.

'At last we're firmly braking, and wheezing in slow motion:
Signal arms are beckoning, as we read them with devotion,
And clank along the junctions, our sweaty drivers showing
A weary face to passengers, with soot on cheeks reposing,
Leaning tiredly out of cab-doors to finish off their story,
As we hiss at buffers, with passengers out-pouring,
And cool our boilers quietly, before we go next to Oban…
Before we go next to Oban…Before we go next…to Oban…
Sssssssssssssssss…..zzzzzzzzzzzzzzzzzzzzzz….'

ENGINE DRIVER

I see him still, that craggy driver,
At journey's end, leaning out
Of the cab window, his elbows
Resting, holding his weary body,
Black soot-marks on his cheeks,
Grime on his forehead, his jacket
Still blue but stained with dust,
And that black cap with shiny top
Somehow adding a glimmer of majesty
To a hard job, keeping that dirty brute –
With gloved hand on the regulator –
Trundling at forty-fifty miles per hour
On a straight stretch, four-five miles
Per weary hour on the 1/50 gradients
With heavy, harsh-blasting, choking
Barks of black smoke and steam.
Well done, man of metallic toil,
With that strong jaw and pitted skin!

The fireman still damps down –
I catch glimpses of his forehead,
Flames reflected on his red face,
Shadows playing as he draws the fire,
Perspiration flowing, no time yet
To look out of the victorious cab,
To let passengers admire
His soot-laurelled brow.

Without him, the driver
Could not lean supreme
Gazing through the steam
At Buchanan Street.

BALQUHIDDER

Fifty years later, the name takes me there:
Every time I hear it, hot steam still hisses
From the dome-valve of the 'Black Five',
Heavy doors slam, a walking lantern flashes
Wavering light across a gravel platform,
A voice shouts 'BAL-QUHIDDER',
Some travellers leave the train,
Crunch their feet on the cracked stones,
Walk away, but we journey on,
As a whistle blows, and a green lamp
Swings permission to the driver
To release the brake and fill hard cylinders
From the boiler's blazing energy.

We heave ourselves up Glen Ogle,
A slow, heavy haul, with orange sparks
From the chimney flying backwards,
Leaving a smoking trail in the heather:
They will see it through Strathyre.

This corridor coach is humid in the night
As we head for Killin Junction:
My mother talks to Faith Mission pilgrims
On their way to be fishers of men in Tiree:
One of them from Lewis speaks Gaelic,
Her strong face intense, its gneiss lines
Accentuated by soft light in the carriage.

This journey is soul-searching, and I want out
To taste sulphur, feel ash on my face
For myself, but that is not ordained:
I can't endure tweed prickles in my skin
In this over-heated oven with boiling narratives.

With my finger, I draw a boat
On the moisture of the window-pane,
Where breath's hot air has condensed creatively:
I fashion an image of the *Claymore*,
Its hull dripping wet, running with streams,
Anticipating tomorrow's voyage from Oban.

We creak to a harsh halt on the bay's edge;
Mast-lights bedeck the star-clouded sky:
Heavy doors slam in leaden discord:
The salt, seagull-laden sea air blasts
Through that pressure-cooker carriage,
Lowering the temperature:
Gulping, I step into refreshing freedom
As the 'Black Five' hisses
At the buffers.

STRATHYRE

(In grateful imitation of Edward Thomas, 'Adlestrop'.)

Yes, I remember Strathyre,
The name, because one afternoon
Of mist a 'Black Five' drew up there
Wontedly. It was late June.

The steam hissed. Someone cleared his throat.
A few left and a few came
On the bare platform. What I saw
Was that marble heron – without name,

And flower-beds, shrubs and grass,
And gravelly edges, trimmed and dry,
But that bird was no less still and lonely fair
Than on a Tiree shore, rigid against the sky,

And in that minute a passenger sang
'Bonnie Strathyre', and round him mistier,
Farther and farther, all the singers
Of Perthshire and Argyllshire.

OBAN EXILE

OBANTOWN MORNING

The Seekers sing again;
Oban comes to mind;
Mary 'Myrtle Bank',
Queen of all things kind:

At breakfast that song plays,
And Judith sets the day:
Down Ardconnel Road,
I walk towards the bay.

Rockin', rollin', ridin',
Columba in from Mull:
Carrying hopes and fears,
Cars within her hull.

King George raises steam,
Sleek beauty of her day,
Prepares to carry seekers
Many miles away.

Somewhere they will find
Sunshine for their soul:
Iona, isle of saints,
Is their spirits' goal.

Claymore lurches round,
Avoiding Corran Ledge,
Tiree within her plates,
Vibes in every edge:

Rockin', rollin, ridin',
Round the isles they go:
Somewhere harbour beckons
Seekers we all know.

Oban Exile

MARY 'MYRTLE BANK'

Though I should spend a lifetime
Reflecting on the days
I spent upon my wanders
In education's ways,
In Oban and in Glasgow,
And Cambridge for a phase,
The digs I had with Mary
Will merit all my praise.

However high your standing, however low your rank,
You'd always get a welcome from Mary 'Myrtle Bank'.

Mary's lovely villa
Was truly quite a place,
When you had climbed Ardconnel
With a very weary pace:
Mary would be standing
With a smile upon her face,
To tell you she'd been waiting
To let you have some space.

'Myrtle Bank's' expansion
Was built in every wall:
No matter who should seek it,
Rooms were there for all:
Close beside the Tower,
It stood up fair and tall,
With plants in every window,
And two dogs in the hall.

When Mary laid her table,
Its legs would almost break,
With all the food upon it –
Bread and cheese and cake:
Mary would be cooking,
And sometimes she would bake
The finest, largest pancakes
And sweetest chocolate flake.

There was Charlie there, and Norrie
From Tobermory Bay,
And Charlie Ives from Sunart,
And MacDonalds the same way:
And John MacLeod the banker,
With fresh wit every day,
To laugh at all the lodgers
And guarantee they'd pay.

Adventures there were many,
Going down the town at night,
When cops would find the laddies,
And think it wasn't right
That they were buying matches
To keep their fags alight –
Aye, yon was quite a household,
And every day was bright.

Mary, she was happy,
Without a frown or stare,
Except when her poor doggies
Were pushed off a cosy chair:
Woe betide the fellow
Who'd put them out of there –
The dogs were just so precious,
And lived on first-class fare.

Oh, Mary, she was special,
And never did I stay
In such a happy household
As I had by Oban Bay!
I'll ever hear her laughter,
I'll always give her praise;
Her smile will never leave me
Till I conclude my days.

LAST ASSEMBLY

(In memory of John Maclean (1909–70),
Rector of Oban High School, 1950–66.)

Strange how I am still there,
Rector, bidding you farewell,
As you stand at that lonely lectern
For the last time, unassuming,
Your words clear in my memory,
'And I am wearing my gown
To show that I am going down
Fighting.'

That gentle smile each morning
As you stood watching each pupil,
Your quiet pride from a warm heart,
Guiding their young ways,
Keeping that fatherly eye,
Rejoicing to see strong people
Coming up life's stairs:
'It is good to be clever,
But it is better to be nice.'

You held on to that gown
With both hands:
I will see you for ever,
With that slight list
As the breeze caught
Your fading sail
In the Sound of
Raasay.

For me you will
Never go down.

Nor will the lump
In my throat
At that last assembly.

SPREADING WINGS

FIRST FLIGHT FROM TIREE
on a BEA Pionair / Dakota 1961

She sits back on her tail,
Relaxed, glittering in sunshine,
Nose high above hangars
Of black-rusted metal,
Huge doors open,
Fire-tender poised;
Aluminium aircraft
Trimmed in crimson,
Arrogantly aloof,
Knowing she can fly
Above dark restriction,
Unfettered by enclosure.

I clamber up the steep aisle,
Swimming through chairs
Of redolent red leather,
Find my window seat,
Show my lapel badge
As an unaccompanied child
To the flight attendant;
Passengers arrive, fasten
Adult straps for adventure,
Indifferent to the boy.

Sinews tighten as we taxi out,
Piston engines blasting smoke,
Frames vibrating on the runway,
When she turns lurchingly round;
Then, engines roaring,
She sets off sluggishly,
Heavily, ponderously,
Wings imperfectly coordinated
Pulling reluctant wheels,
Her tail rising grudgingly,
Slowly parallel to ground,
Ungainly Dakota elevating
Her obstinate body,
Snubbing black hangars,
Heaving hard against gravity.

Rivets rattle as we leave
Crossapol Bay banking
In evening gentleness;
I watch Tiree fading,
Reef runway shrinking,
Silver wings holding
Future immensities,
Thundering towards
A sharply clear horizon
Of harsh mountains.

SISTER JEAN KENNEDY

De Havilland Heron G-ANXA, *Sister Jean Kennedy*, was acquired by Scottish Airways in 1953, and, with her sister G-ANXB, *Sir James Young Simpson*, served the Hebrides and Scotland with distinction until 31 March 1973. Both Herons were closely associated with air ambulance flights throughout the country, including Tiree, as recalled gratefully in this poem. The *Sister Jean Kennedy* was named in honour of Sister Jean Kennedy from Coll, who died on board another Heron aircraft which crashed in bad weather on an ambulance flight to Islay in 1957.

Engines roar overhead,
Down she sweeps,
Navigation lights flashing,
Aluminium bird,
Cockpit silhouettes,
Peaked caps,
Main tyres bite tarmac
Of flat Reef,
Nose-wheel touches,
Throttles ease back,
The rudder flaps,
Captain follows routing
To the apron,
Engines whir to stop,
Propellers secured,
Chocks on wheels.

Steps go alongside,
Door opens,
Red-caped nurse walks down,
Patient stretchered over,
Carried on board,
Care in charge.
Door closed.

Pilots write logs,
Captain looks out.
No time to lose,
Gets 'All clear',
Waves gloved hand.

We stand back,
Chocks away,
Propellers rotate,
Slicing air, transparent circles,
Silver in dark night.
She turns tail over my head –
I've never been so close –
Rudder flapping momentarily,
Lights flashing starboard green,
Port wing-tip crimson,
Underside beacon white,
Glitter of airport lamps
On undulating fuselage.

Elegant in emergency,
She taxies off gently
Down to runway,
Turns to position,
Opens full throttle,
Makes a dash for the sky,
Ascending steeply.

Lights fade out over the sea,
But hope now sparkles
In the darkness.

Indelible image,
Memory vibrant,
Deathless 'Sister Jean',
Unforgettable Heron of mercy,
Heroine of Hebridean sacrifice.

THE TWIN OTTER SONG

The Twin Otter is a flyer
That will never let you down:
She will keep you up aloft
When weather wears a frown:
When the ferry's stuck in Oban,
And storms are raging round,
That trusty wee Twin Otter
Will rise above their sound.

You'll see that splendid aircraft
When you walk about a mile
Along the lengthy corridors
Of Glasgow Airport's pile:
When you're about to falter
And feel you need a smile,
The grin from yon wee Otter
Will make it all worthwhile.

You'll step aboard with gladness,
Find the buckle on the seat,
Pull it out and fasten it,
Making sure your belt is neat:
Then the officer will tell you
You'll really get a treat:
Cloud is thick as porridge,
But the journey will be sweet.

They will take you to the islands
Over rivers, lochs and hills:
You'll see your native Scotland
In a way that always thrills:
As you soar away from Glasgow,
You'll marvel at the drills
Of First Officer and Captain
With their VisitScotland skills.

They'll take you over Cowal,
Past Crinan and Loch Fyne,
Across yon Coire Bhreacain,
With its angry, swirling brine:
By Lorn and Loch Linnhe,
Past Mull that's always fine,
With big Ben More to starboard,
And Iona west in line.

And soon you'll be descending
To the island that you know:
You'll see the huge Ben Hynish
With its Golf Ball out for show:
There's Scarinish and Caolas,
And Gunna Sound's bright glow,
To fill your heart with gladness,
As you touch the Reef below.

You'll hear the throttles easing
When the Otter's on the ground:
She'll purr with satisfaction
That you are safe and sound:
She'll say, 'Tis my great pleasure
To know that I have found
The most splendid little airport
For many miles around.'

Ah yes, yon wee Twin Otter
Is the jewel of the skies:
From the Arctic to the Pampas,
They know she really flies:
On ice sheets or on machair,
Whatever be their size,
Whatever wind or weather,
The Otter wins the prize.

TIREE LANDING, DECEMBER 2014

Runway becomes insecure,
Lurching this way and that,
Leaping sideways, jumping,
Rising and falling, detached
From solid machair,
Unpredictable.

Will it condescend
To meet the Twin Otter
In forty-knot wind?
Will she finally
Decide to mate
With it in this
Defiant dance
Of elemental
Relationships?

Hand raised
Gripping throttles
Pilot coaxes her
Downwards
Dipping deeply
Through waves
Of stormy emotion.

Then at last
With reluctance
Tyres kiss concrete,
Lungs releasing
Tight breath.

Airport tender
Deftly lies across
Otter's blunt nose:
No taxi-ing today
Except in the
Land Rover.

At the Terminal
We wave wanly to
Departing passengers
In lashing rain.

HOMECOMING, MAY 2016

G-SGTS spreads light wings wide
Over the west end of Coll, Crossapol,
Caolas of white lips, Gunna chewing
Quietly into a curdle of edging salt,
Its solitary cottage dotted on the eye,
An Caolas Bàn between islands
Where lively lythe double-hooked
Themselves on lines in my hands,
Almost pulling me into the surge
All of fifty years ago; they will have
Grown so much bigger by now,
Those lythe of memory's sea.

Wing dips to port as we follow
The hidden beam over the Sound;
I feel it guiding me, as I watch
Familiar outlines sharpening,
Caolas shorelines, rocks, islands,
Greasamul rising to meet me
With a laser so powerful
That I am dazzled, blinded
By such intrusive immediacy
As I see notched shorelines
Become roads of the mind
Leading to homes, while yonder
At the junction of two roads –
Or is it three or four? –
Sits that gale-gabled house,
Distant yet utterly immediate,
Still defiant, determined,
Radiating signals that guide
My heart into raging storms
Of tranquillity and terror.

No neutrality in the pulse
Of this returning never-leaver,
This commuting native-exile
Trapped between worlds,
Struggling to rise above
The downdrag of reality,
Glad to sense it all again,
That magnetism undying
With conflicting polarities.

We lose height gradually
Over May-grassed machairs,
Wind-turbine waving welcoming
Arms above the graveyard,
Gott Bay of many partings,
Multitudinous arrivals
Between its massive arms.

I turn to look back
As rubber wheels whack
The tarmac runway,
Solidly indifferent
To this latest landing.

It is a hard homecoming
Always. Who cares?
I think I may have
Returned again,
But where am I
And who?

SPREADING WINGS

FAITH IN
COMMUNITY

TUNE 'GLASGOW'

Back I go to Balemartine,
My father on the bridge
Of that plain church,
Neil MacArthur steering
Our musical course,
Cadences like waves
On the shore outside,
Some swirling the sand,
Some barely noticeable
In the cacophonous
Harmony of souls
On board this lively tune.

I imagine the Mountain
Of the Lord, rising
As high as Ben Hynish
Or just a little higher,
Perhaps as high as
Ben Nevis on the horizon
On a good clear day.

I struggle with yon wave of doggerel,
Deploring the crowds of slain,
Hosts encountering hosts,
Verbal conflicts by the score,
Crying for interpretation
But meriting burial.

I imagine the trumpet hanging
Like some discarded flotsam
On an unsteady clothes-peg
In the unfinished internal porch;
I envy those privileged pupils
Who study 'War No More'
When I have to stew
Over algebra.

Heavy with incomprehensible cargo,
We lurch into the next stanza,
Barely coping with the swell,
Neil struggling with the tiller:
Through the welcome window
I see mist between me and Mull,
Ben More hidden in cloud.

BALEPHUIL

Tràigh Bhì spanning white ahead,
Its waves washing the windscreen,
Ceann a' Bharra a warm hump,
Loch a' Phuill lying low to my right
As I bring those saints home
From the Balemartine service;
The red kiosk on that gable
Talks as I open the sliding-door,
Telephone wires humming beyond.

They leave with hymns of gratitude;
Màiri Flòraidh has been 'safely landed',
Eilidh Sheumais says, 'Thank you, a luaidh',
Dòmhnall a' Mhinistir leans nasally
Into the stiff wind, his coat flapping,
Mrs MacKay steers her lively brood
Down the brae to the Bail' Ùr;
I then drive on with Teen
In her plastic raincoat, stooped,
Becoming old now, but still
Shining with godly radiance,
Her appreciation flowing
In gifts of unforgettable books,
A beautiful hope in her eye;
I leave her at the Cùiltean,
Watch her on the road edge.

Then I too turn homewards,
Glimpsing Skerryvore's pillar
Ever holding fast in storms;
I see boats safe among rocks,
Drive the Bedford slowly over
Those gentle braes, view the loch
Clear below, and thank God for
Balephuil, 'Baile nan Gràs',
Township of Divine Grace:
I met angels there –
And I look forward
To the next time.

RUAIG CHURCH 'SOCIAL'

Evangelicals have their hair down
In that old church in Ruaig tonight:
Keen to kill formality except in the pulpit,
The community arrives for some fun:
Listens bravely until the tea-therapy
At half-time, when fairy-cake shrapnel flies,
Precision-guided into Lachie Cameron's cup,
Throwing a tidal-wave into his saucer:
Laughter explodes from my licked lips,
As another missile soars archly overhead,
Descending neatly on the guest speaker,
Right on his pate, as he looks heavenwards:
Huge teapots are held by serious ladies
Who now smile as they serve tables,
Fulfilling roles and filling rolls,
In the eternal kitchen fitted for them:
It's our way in the aisles.

Favourite hymns are sung gustily,
On a stormy night within, without:
Eilidh Sheumais's soaring solo awaited,
Her party piece, with customary preface,
'Tha mi làn a-nochd (I am full tonight)':
She launches, high-pitched, into the waves
Of flowing emotion, glistening eyes,
Sails bravely through twenty-five Gaelic verses,
Avoiding jagged sharps, quavering occasionally,
Grace notes buoying notes of grace,
Until she reaches harbour on a high tide,
Voices joining in the spiritual shanty,
The long voyage over.

Sanctified spontaneity overflows,
Order of Service barely holding course,
As children take the stage, bring plays,
Go through recitations, forget words,
Adult whispers, faith faltering:
Drama wraps it up, drives it,
Paradoxically playful,
Evangelical anarchy,
Mystic mutinies
On the old ship of Zion.

Cailean Lachainn preaches tall,
Having pranced into the pulpit,
Takes the helm as pilot,
Steadies ship and passengers,
Dark suit and white-starched collar,
Charting out the broad and narrow roads:
Rhetorical righteousness reigns
Temporarily at the heart of happiness:
Choices to be made, can't have both:
But both are here tonight:
Sunday service subverted.

In fact, a chàirdean, tonight we have
A broad church sailing on the broad road,
To self-reinforcement, not destruction,
As a community revels freely,
Throws off its shackles, breaks chains,
In the glinting lamplight of hard walls,
Expresses deep desires, pent-up powers,

FAITH IN COMMUNITY

Rejoices on both sides of the threshold,
Continues on corporate pilgrimage
With its feet now on dry land,
Shows the church who's boss:

'We're marching to Zion,
Beautiful, beautiful, Zion:
We're marching upward to Zion,
The beautiful city of God.'

GOD'S HOUSE?

Strange to think that God
Lived in that house once:
He was utterly extravagant:
He put on all the lights
For a whole month,
Which made the east end
Sit up and take notice.

There was no electricity then,
Only Tilley lamps hissing,
But God's light blazed out
In a dazzling revival.
Many who went there
Saw that light, walked home
Illumined for ever.

Odd, though, that the light
Faded, and the walls of glory
Became desolate: Ichabod.
They began to disintegrate,
Fall apart, door ever open
To receive cattle.

Tainted as the sole trustee,
Faithless in my stewardship,
I had to sell God's house
In case it killed folk
In the darkness of
A devilish storm.

Now, as I pass, I see
A faint light in a window:
I feel that some day soon
I must knock on that door
To ask if God has
Come home.

CHAPEL IN AURORA

You were in your element that night,
Stars singing dazzling songs above you,
Cosmic strobe-lights spreading greens, blues,
Yellows, oranges across the heavens,
Your walls illumined with gladness.

You seemed to belong to that display,
To feel its kinship within your mortar,
Rediscovering your otherworldliness
As the Aurora Borealis danced
Throughout the praising sky.

I suspect you too felt much lighter
When you found humans inside you
Once again: perhaps your new role
Linked with greater purposes
In that glorious spectacle.

LAST SERVICE AT KIRKAPOL
8 December 2013

Did I live through that? Was I there?
Or was it a phantom of the night,
Come to create a false grieving?
It lurks in the depths
Where no ordinary chores
Or routine memories linger, where
Reality lies behind necessary facade.

My fingers press keys reluctantly
On this board, and they translate
Into faint music in the far corner,
Organ cowering under supreme pulpit,
Playing a soft, final tune,
As the weighty Bible is carried
Solemnly downwards, step by step,
By an east-end Elder, no Word
Left on the book-board.

The font follows into a morning of mist,
And then the congregation drags itself
From the sanctuary into the cramped vestibule,
The sea grey today, the sky downcast,
Gott Bay's sweeping crescent ready to accept,
In gusting winds, that sighing in the soul.

I stand uneasily, trying to converse,
My mind asking if this is the remnant
Of night's silly turmoil, brain's chaos,
An outline devoid of substance,
But somehow it remains, pushes itself at me,
Tells me that it has happened,
But I deny it a hearing.

That fortress of reformed faith,
Squarely obstinate, stubborn in the gales,
Rose above the glowering clouds
As I drove through the cold puddles
Of night's ceaseless downpours.
The island landmark bulked before me,
Massive block of parish authority,
Steering life from conception
To eternal resurrection.
So it must endure:
As then on a million occasions,
So now and for ever more.
But this is terminal, an ending,
No hope of physical resurrection
For this almighty building.

FAITH IN COMMUNITY

Another parish church stands empty,
Successor to St Columba's ancestral chapel,
Now a roofless ruin in the graveyard,
Doorless with gaping gables, frail fabric finite,
Rev. Neil MacLean mere dust in the western corner,
Replicating the last pilgrimages of a myriad mortals,
Whose births, marriages and deaths it recorded,
Directed, consecrated, commemorated,
On their journeys across life's machair,
Over these very roads to Kirkapol,
Sun and rain, calm and storm, joy and sorrow,
Until they ended there.

That great cloud of witnesses
Conveys me homeward,
And lingers until now.
Presences remain, talking, arguing,
Singing, preaching, praying,
Pressing themselves hard
Upon my fruitless frailty:

That locked door, they say,
Is not real, for faith continues:
But I was there, and I saw and felt
Another painful conclusion.

SKY SURFER

This morning, on the way to church,
I saw the huge Skysurfer leaping in the air,
Catching the wind, going where it listed,
Crossing the clouds, then round again,
Dancing above waves, heaving a man
Backwards and forwards, seemingly
At the mercy of time and tide,
Out of control, minnow caught
By a force above his strength
On the long waves of Gott Bay.

Yet he had mastered
What I have never learned:
His limbs flexing,
Whirling in response
To God's mighty breeze,
An equilibrium
Of body and spirit.

Me? I'm terrified
To try: I drive cautiously
Along the road, the wheel
Firmly clutched in my hands,
Engine under my predictable control,
Disapprovingly watching others
Celebrating new harmonies
With ancient elements.

SHORE LINES

NEWCOMERS

GEESE

What birds are these that thickly flock upon my fields,
As if they had some right to claim the grass,
And crop it back until the earth protrudes?
What gives them power to find their way across
From Greenland's barren shores and restless seas
To vex the tranquil pastures of my mind?

I hear their calls, as they come clouding down,
Leave their arrow-long formation and alight,
With browns and greys and stabs of white,
Creating rugged ridges roving over soil.

For years, they did not come, nor did I hear
Their squawks or wingbeats on the morning air.
Now on the green, broad machair they spread out
In waddling, weighty lumps that catch my eye.

They are impostors, they should not be here,
So let me blast them upwards, feather-bomb the sky,
Fragment them to the heavens whence they've come,
As on the fields of Normandy the enemy flew apart
As tunnelled munitions exploded hand and foot and heart.

How strange! How violent these creatures make my yen!
Yet now I drop my gun – and net them with my pen!

FAIR TIREE

(With apologies to W.B. Yeats.)

I will arise and drive now, and drive to fair Tiree,
And a beautiful 'croft' build there, of Velux windows made:
A huge felt roof will I have there, and a dish for Sky TV,
And live alone in one bee-loud gale.

But I'll not have any peace there, as peace doesn't want to know,
With the croaking of the corncrake, in the morning when it sings:
There midnight's all a daze, that bird's still on the go,
And evening's full of my iPad's pings.

I will arise and drive now, as always night and day,
I hear the rain-storm lashing with loud sounds by the door:
While I queue in the Co-op, or drown surfing in Gott Bay,
I feel a yen for Tenerife in the deep heart's core.

WORD FOR WINDOWS

We build our houses with windows,
We answer aesthetical calls;
Nature's Grand Views attract us,
We have no time for walls.

As long as we see the sunset,
And say 'Ooh' and 'Aah' as it palls,
We get the essence of islands –
We don't need to bother with walls!

We see the maahvellous mountains,
The quaint little cottage with stalls,
Where the natives kept their animals,
But we do not need such walls!

We are the new generation,
With speedboats and trailers and balls;
We play around on the beaches,
And build our house without walls!

The sand is our finest foundation,
The rocks are the place for the trolls;
We know for a fact that we're winning –
Our edifice never falls!

JOLLY JOGGER

I am the jolly jogger,
And I jog around Tiree,
On machairs, yes and mountains,
And down beside the sea.

I love the island breezes,
They really make me fly,
And if you see me levitate,
Now you will know why!

It is this joyful summer,
With a friendly wee Force Six,
And heavy rain to show me
How best to move my sticks!

From Balephuil to Caolas,
And all townships in between,
You might see Mary Poppins –
That's me above your screen!

For when you are a-driving,
I'll be up there on high,
Listening to my iPod,
And looking from the sky!

I may not even see you
As I land upon the road,
So on that lovely single track,
Make way for me, you toad!

Oh, I'm the jolly jogger,
And on and on I go,
A-skipping round your island –
So now I hope you know!

POLYTUNNEL PERSPECTIVE

Now I understand it, in this
Place of false perspiration:

Those people who always say
'How lovely!', 'So nice!',
'Beautiful!', 'Wonderful!',
Whenever I mention Tiree,
That island of hard choices,
Of storms, hail, rain, lightning,
Thunder exploding over roofs,
And occasional good days...

....live in a polytunnel,
Enjoying the microclimate
Of warmed-up ignorance,
Seeing a summer world,
With no unpredictable springs,
No tempestuous autumns,
No wild, withering winters,
Unaware of their own
Plasticated fragility.

People who live in a polytunnel
Should not throw words:
They might some day
Turn into stones.

ENCOUNTERS

Walking is intuitive here,
Old ley-lines guiding the feet
In magnetic paths, earth's energies
Amplified by centuries
Of knowledgeable contact.
They lead to the locations
Of houses deeply rooted in me,
But now rebuilt new-style
For people with no familiarity,
Sitting on the edge of sand-blow.

They watch me through huge doors
Of glass, worried that a native
Has come with his dogs,
Unkempt, wind blowing his jacket
Across their designer minds.
Anxiety needs no words.
What is he doing here?
We each sense Other.

I divert shorewards
Remembering the ferrymen
Who fought this liminality,
Pulling on huge oars, eloquent
Storytellers of Gunna Sound,
Blustery today, waves looking
Hostile, but manageable,
Easily navigated if needed
With the dipping lug.

I glimpse above sharp marram
A yellow surfboard on a car roof,
Totem of a new devotion,
Colourful kites hauling
Their owners religiously
To their extreme heaven.
Their god does the divine
Wave classic on the clouds.

On track homewards,
Atavistic meditation
Turns me into another being:
Ley-lines (you don't believe in them?)
Go international instantly:

I am the ghost of Cuavatemoc
Risen out of the Aztec soil
To disturb the dreams of Cortes,
Silent behind glass
Upon a sand-dune in Tiree.

TILLEY THE TIREE TURBINE

Tilley the Tiree turbine
Has a very shapely pose:
Towering over the moorland –
Her beauty grows and grows:
There on the barren landscape
She's the very whitest rose,
Lifting her arms and waving,
To everyone who goes:

'All you who tilt at windmills,
I'd like you now to know
That some of us can generate
A fine electric flow:
At times we're not productive,
Because the breeze is low,
And we like a little rest-time,
Because we go and go…

O, Tilley the Tiree turbine…

'We also add some colour
To the heather at your door;
The lochs, the rocks and bogland,
Can have a better show:
When blue skies are above us,
We will not be slow;
When the clouds are floating,
They say, "O, Tilley, go…"

O, Tilley the Tiree turbine…

'At night we love the moonshine,
And our red lights will glow;
Then we're like a spaceship,
Wanting to land below:
You can hear us whooping –
That's our best "Hello!"
We're here to make you happy –
To say you're not alone!'

O, Tilley the Tiree turbine…

LOSING THE ISLAND

THE GAZE

Blessed are those who have the Gaze
As they walk the tourist ways,
Tramp the pathways through the hills,
Reach the peaks and see the thrills,
Go by valleys, straths and glens,
Admire the ruined but-and-bens,
Before heading far out west
To apply the Gaze to all that's best;
'Fantastic, fabulous!' they cry,
As the appeal is to the eye;
At every rugged shore they reach,
They will shout, 'Life is a beach!'

Now to that island I will go,
Where the visions are below,
Or encased within a mind
That is not the tourist kind;
One that does not have a Gaze
To sweep across the empty bays;
One that knows, and one that sees,
A world of people – but not these!
For they have gone, and here am I,
Gazing at a darkened sky.

THE REALITY

'Sunsets and sunrises are our islands,
Our pleasure-zones, our Nirvanas,
Where we discover ourselves,
The truth, the reality.'

Ah yes! That rings a bell!
My reality dawned over
The Sound of Gunna a while ago
On a chill winter's morning,
And since then I've been seeing
Gaps left by storms, tidal erosion,
Sand-blow encroaching steadily,
Seaweed strewn across roads,
Plastic bottles, nylon ropes,
Black streamers on fences
That nobody bothers to remove,
Rubbish flying across machairs,
Old cars bedecking landscapes,
Rusting implements, houses chewed
By wind and rain, desolated by death.

I can ignore some sharp-edged objects,
Mere material that I don't want to see:
But harder by far are the gaps
In the community that I once knew,
The funerals, the visits to homes
Where bereavement has struck,
The locked doors, the transformed
Commonality that now I do not know:

LOSING THE ISLAND

A brutal sense of strangeness
Invades my own shorelines;
I am made for yesterday,
A native alien in terra cognita:
Like Ossian after the Fianna,
Glad when I meet survivors
From my own generation
With Gaelic on their lips.

Ah yes! I've discovered
My own reality in the changing sky –
It's a damnable dawning of the self –
And in the long, long evening,
A searing sunset shedding gold braid
Over darkening fields,
Beguiling beauty
In a graveyard.

Who can rescue me
From my island
Of self-discovery?
Where can I find
Home?

HOME?

When we 'go home' to islands,
Where do we find that 'home'?
In people, place or deep within
A creatively driven part of self
Powered by delusion?

A delusion that is concrete,
Firm and tangible, until we touch
Fragments from the past
And find no more than dust
Upon our fingers: the place
Alien, remade by others,
Ever disintegrating,
Our people gone.

Regardless we live loyally
In devoted denial,
Negotiating the particles
Past, present and future
In that broken breached
Continuum of the mind,

Reciting verbal therapy
As we travel
Never arriving
But always there,
Ever returning nowhere,
Selfless exiles,
Fearing nothing.

EXILE

We no longer need to cross oceans
In coffin-ships to become exiles,
Nor do we need to endure Glasgow
Of the dark satanic mills (of old)
Or even brick-brown Manchester
With those emaciated matchstick-folk,
Sky-scraping chimneys lowrying
Above their desiccated souls.

We are much better-off now
With car-ferries, not coffin-ships;
So we can return, even stay,
Spend our exiles at home,
Crusoes of the crofts
Surrounded by new worlds
Of ghostly intrusions,
Listen to alien accents
Telling novel tales
For our instruction –
But not in Gaelic.

We can be spooked daily
By that relentless rumble
Of bull-barred vehicles
With red surf-boards on roofs,
White-camper-van people
Striding hard across machairs,
Their sinless dogs leashless,
Island under their feet,
Our croft their croft,
Roaming rightly.

Let's raise a grateful glass
To this ease of exile:
It has come to us:
We can reach Essex
By driving to Crossapol.
Skerryvore is now
Our Statue of Liberty.

OLD MILL

It grinds my emotions
With its inert drive-wheel,
Immobile against the flow
Of the lively surging lade,
Ceaseless survivor
Of deathless decay,
Still available for service
For those with hearts
To channel it effectively,

Ears to hear once again
The flap of those floats,
The whirl of agile axles
On oiled gear-wheels,
Huge querns trundling,
White flour spilling
On storytellers' feet
In purposeful profusion,
Miller holding forth.

Today I see no miller,
No line of carting crofters,
Nothing for the great stones
To pound into smooth meal
For the bread of Gaelic life:
Nourishment lies elsewhere,
Indifferent lorries delivering
Sacks of ready-made mash
Purloined from smooth
Mainland merchants.

My girnal is almost empty,
Waiting for the jagged grain
Of rare home-grown memory
To ripen on the hard ears
Of barbed barley, sprouting
In spite of deadly storms
Of packaged complicity.

In the old mill's shadow,
I bow gladly on my knees
To grind my scarce crop
Against that other grain.

HISTORY

You're just off the boat, aren't you?
Well, just let me prepare you
For living here for a few days.

There were natives here once,
Primitive people with the Gaelic,
Not terribly worldly-wise, you know,
A bit simple, and they died out,
Apart from the occasional oddity
Who speaks the lingo and writes
Poems that nobody else understands:
You can go to the Yohlan
To read about their customs,
If you really need to know,
If you really care:

Mercifully somebody
Had enough wisdom
To shove the past
Into storage.
A wise move,
On the whole,
Wouldn't you say?

Now, where was I? Oh yes,
We came to fill gaps with hyphens,
To extend our sunny summers,
To rebuild the tumble-down
Walls and ruins, replace them
With super mod-con cottages,
Prize-winning black houses,
To live the stormless dream,
To escape our self-made nightmares,
To get away from all that stress,
To go native globally
In our very local way –
By taking it all
To Tiree.

So here we are, doing fine
As you can see, but always
Pleased when someone comes
To keep up the connection
With the old home.
How are they all
Back in Billericay?

EROSION

Strange how communities vanish
Before our noses, but we don't notice,
As one light goes off, and then another,
And a lock is turned for the last time,
Even by our own hands. The winter
Cloak of darkness becomes warmer
As we watch Sky TV and shut out
The emptiness that lies within a mile,
The holes in the heart of life.

Nor do we perceive rising sea-levels
As they eat rocks quietly, continuously,
Stormily, seeing only calm days of long
Deceitful peace which we affirm
As reality in our island.

Not until we take the road
To the story that we heard
And now admire – too late –
And seek for deeper sense,
Do we reach the graveyard
Of our dearest thought.

We'll get back home safely:
The roadmen have repaired
The breach made by the tide
When it carried off silently
A hundred feet of tarmac
Without our knowing.

Perhaps we'll waken up
The day a township
Falls right over,
And takes us
With it.

HOLIDAYS?

'How are you enjoying your holidays?'
I bridle instantly, incensed, repressing
Welling emotions, feeling strafed
By friendly native fire, kindly meant;
I wonder what they think we were doing
Over thirty years of summers and springs
In the family's labour-camp, our gulag,
Heaving out the rubbish of generations,
Grappling with the luggage of the past,
Emptying outhouses and garrets
Of blankets, clothes, shrouds, linen,
Wielding brushes of whitewash and paint,
Replacing locks, immovable with rust,
Keeping doors from rotting with rain,
Preserving crumbling lime and weathered stone,
Plastering the cracks, maintaining windows –
The list is endless.

'How are you enjoying your holidays?'
Let me tell you gently that I am pleased
That the house stood until another member
Of the family came and gutted the inside
With our blessing, support, goodwill;
And now I sit in a restored room
Marvelling at what has happened;
Enjoyment is not the word
For a struggle to preserve
Ancient loyalties.

So let me tell you too, dear friend:
If we had gone to Tenerife or Lanzarote,
Or to New York or the Costa del Sol,
On a holiday with no thought
For duties or responsibilities
To the home of my people,
I would not have been here today
To bridle at your polite concern.

The holiday is yet to be,
But we are nearly there.
It will surely be worth
The thirty-year delay.
I feel it already
In my bones.

LOSING THE ISLAND

REFLECTIONS ON
THE EDGE

WHEN I FEEL OLD

When I feel old, I do not seek your pity
Or even my own: I find the well-worn path
That leads to the shore, and there,
Gazing across to Coll and Mull, I admire
Vast ages beyond my conception.

I stand humbly, the tiniest, youngest speck
Of sand upon that beach, raised gradually
Through aeons beyond my calculation
Upon a solid multi-posted bed of stone.
Those rocks, heated in white-hot furnaces,
Pounded, pulverised by primordial pressures,
Sedimentary, bulldozed to become metamorphic,
Some two hundred and fifty million years ago,
Give or take ten million here or there. What's that
Between geological friends? See that black rock
Which somehow forced itself cheekily
Between layers of two billion year-old gneiss?
Well, it came out of Ben More a mere sixty million
Years ago, when Vulcan owned the show,
And forced his igneous way across
What is now below that eternal spread of sea,
Which wasn't there at the time – it's very recent.
Sometimes I imagine the *Clansman* sailing
Through waves of magma, a blazing fire-brand
Of white sparks at her bow, her wake petrifying!
I'm glad that water came to cool things down,
To make life easier for CalMac.

Sedimentary, metamorphic, igneous – I know little
About any of them. I can only stand there, look
And marvel to the best of my inability.
Then I turn away, my step lighter, my mind
At the very beginning of youth's enquiry.
Old, did I say? Old? OLD?
I've hardly been born!
I'm still in rompers!

SEAL MORNING

(In memory of Zac.)

That last morning we are at Port an t-Sruthain,
Zac, nine seals' heads appeared in the grey bay,
Blunt, black heads pointing sharp whiskers right at us,
Swimming until they almost stranded on the ebb,
Just to get a good look at us – me, you, and Mya.

It made me feel uneasy, but as you sniffed the sand,
Going round the edges of the rocks with pulsating tail,
And Mya leapt into the silk-frothed spread of tide,
They became our friends, no more than part
Of that sweeping harmony of vast being.

Then as we walked up the track, they turned away,
Knowing that they would not see us three any more.

Or so I thought once, but now I understand:
They saw beyond Mya and me, and focused on you,
Remembering the day you played with them,
Hide-and-seek out to Greasamul, and you so seal-like,
And all of us laughing our heads into salt tears.
As they led you a merry dance by disappearing:

Now I am sure they were inviting you
To play with them again –
For ever, and for real.

TIREE IMAGES

(Another for Kenneth Steven.)

Tiree is a regatta of white houses
Tacking in a green wind;

Its sounds are a crested chorus
Of conflicting waters;

Its bays are a glitter of cowries
Edged with distant mountains;

Its skies are radiant infinities
Showered with birdsong;

Its machairs are pages of sand
Planted with indelible memory;

Its townships are scattered jewels
On a ring of salted silver.

ISLAND ON THE FAR HORIZON

Island on the far horizon,
Many, many miles away,
Distant, misty, and invisible –
Not to those who know your sway!

Island on the far horizon
Means a brochure holiday,
Lazy, listless, unconnected –
Not for those who feel your sway!

Island on the far horizon,
Evening dreams in sunset ray,
Black on gold now silhouetted –
Not to those who see your sway!

Island close within my being,
Anchored in my deepest clay,
Controlling, holding, all-possessing –
When will I escape your sway?

Back I come to walk the shorelines,
Feel the storms along the bay,
Shaping, moulding with a chisel –
Cutting softest flesh away.

Not for warm romantic daydreams,
Not for idle, endless play,
But in constant, painful vigil,
You demand to have your sway.

SHORE LINES

Sea rips rocks
Spray splashes
Foam on flecked sand

Wave pulls back
Sucked seawards
Hurled headlong hard

Washes my feet
Dog leaps along
Circling on lead

We watch wet
Reflections linger
Footprints lost

We walk warily
On smashed shells
At eternity's edge.